09722

Books are to be ret
the last da

09 DEC 2003

GW01150750

LIBREX —

WOLFRETON SCHOOL LIBRARY
R09722Y0277

WOLFRETON UPPER
SCHOOL LIBRARY

THREE GOTHIC PLAYS

By the same author

FULL LENGTH PLAYS

THE CACTUS GARDEN
JONAH
THE MANIPULATOR
PASSPORT TO FLORENCE
ROSES ROUND THE DOOR

ONE-ACT PLAYS

THE CAGEBIRDS
CHANGE PARTNERS
FUNERAL DANCE
GOING HOME
HONEYMOON EXPRESS
INCIDENT
THE LABORATORY
NOW AND THEN
POINT OF VIEW
RIPPLE IN THE POOL
SILENCE ON THE BATTLEFIELD
SOLDIER FROM THE WARS RETURNING
SPLIT DOWN THE MIDDLE
TWO LEAVES AND A STALK

SKETCHES AND MONOLOGUES

ON STAGE
ON STAGE AGAIN
(including Alison, The End of a Picnic, and Resting Place)

DAVID CAMPTON

Three Gothic Plays
FRANKENSTEIN
USHER
CARMILLA

LONDON
J. GARNET MILLER LTD

FIRST PUBLISHED BY J. GARNET MILLER LTD
IN 1973
PRINTED IN GREAT BRITAIN BY
CLARKE, DOBLE & BRENDON LIMITED, PLYMOUTH
© DAVID CAMPTON 1973

ISBN 85343 531 6

All rights reserved. An acting fee is payable on each and every performance of this play. For information regarding the fee for amateur stage performances, application should be made to the publishers:
EC1N 7SL or to the following agents:

J. Garnet Miller Ltd
10 Station Road Industrial Estate, Colwall, Malvern
Worcestershire WR13 6RN *Telephone:* 01684 540154

Great Britain

Eire:

Australia:	Will Andrade, Box 3111, G.P.O., Sydney, N.S.W. 2001.
Kenya, Uganda and Tanganyika:	Master Play Agencies, P.O. Box 452, Nairobi, Kenya.
New Zealand:	The Play Bureau (N.Z.) Ltd., P.O. Box 3611, Wellington.
South Africa:	Darters (Pty) Ltd., P.O. Box 174, Cape Town.

Applications for all other performances should be made to: ACTAC LTD., 16 Cadogan Lane, London, S.W.1.

"They don't write plays like that any more." This is a common cry from playgoers who can look back to productions of any period more than five years earlier than today. And they are quite right. Fashions change in the theatre almost as quickly as in dress shops. What happened to the wave of verse drama prominent ten years ago, or the semi-Chehovian family comedies of the decade before that? If the climate of the theatre is so unsettled, it is small wonder that plays of a kind popular sixty years ago should have vanished completely. This is just what has happened to costume romance. There was a time when our leading actors—Irving, Tree, Martin Harvey, etc.—made and held their reputations with such flash and fire as "The Scarlet Pimpernel", "Under The Red Robe", "The Only Way". But highly coloured melodrama is now almost entirely neglected, which is a pity because it means that our theatre has lost some of its old excitement. A really live theatre should be able to find room in its repertoire for any kind of play: custard-pie farce, kitchen-sink drama, intellectual goonery—and tuppence-coloured swashbuckling.

However the plays that made the great actor-managers famous are period pieces—not just because they are in costume, but because they were written for actors and audiences of a century ago. Styles of presentation and the outlook of audiences are different now. There would be little point in our reviving an old melodrama except as a museum piece. Instead we have tried to capture the thrill of costume romance, and at the same time present a play for a modern audience. This play was written for this cast, this theatre—and this audience. We hope you all enjoy it.

Programme note for the first production of USHER.

FRANKENSTEIN

DAVID CAMPTON

Frankenstein

*A Gothic Thriller
in Two Acts*

based on a story by
MARY SHELLEY

LONDON
J. GARNET MILLER LTD

FIRST PUBLISHED BY J. GARNET MILLER LTD
IN 1973
PRINTED IN GREAT BRITAIN BY
CLARKE, DOBLE & BRENDON LIMITED, PLYMOUTH
© DAVID CAMPTON 1973

ISBN 85343 532 4

All rights reserved. An acting fee is payable on each and every performance of this play. For information regarding the fee for amateur stage performances, application should be made to the publishers: J. GARNET MILLER LTD., 1-5 Portpool Lane, London, EC1N 7SL or *to the following agents:*

Great Britain:	*J. Garnet Miller Ltd*
Eire:	10 Station Road Industrial Estate, Colwall, Malvern Worcestershire WR13 6RN *Telephone:* 01684 540154
Australia:	Will Andrade, Box 3111, G.P.O., Sydney, N.S.W. 2001.
Kenya, Uganda and Tanganyika	Master Play Agencies, P.O. Box 452, Nairobi, Kenya.
New Zealand:	The Play Bureau (N.Z.) Ltd., P.O. Box 3611, Wellington.
South Africa:	Darters (Pty) Ltd., P.O. Box 174, Cape Town.

Applications for all other performances should be made to: ACTAC LTD., 16 Cadogan Lane, London, S.W.1.

CAST

VICTOR FRANKENSTEIN
HENRI CLERVAL
ELIZABETH
JUSTINE
MME. COUPER
M. CLERVAL SNR.
THE CREATURE

The action takes place in and around a small town in Switzerland. The year is 1817.

Frankenstein was first presented at the Library Theatre, Scarborough on 16th July, 1959, with the following cast:

VICTOR	*William Elmhirst*
HENRI	*Alan Ayckbourn*
ELIZABETH	*Dona Martyn*
JUSTINE	*Faynia Jeffery*
MME. COUPER	*Ann Hughesdon*
M. CLERVAL	*David Campton*
THE CREATURE	*Stephen Joseph*

Directed by *Stephen Joseph*

PRODUCTION NOTE

In the original production of this play the stage was divided into three parts. On one side was the apparatus of Frankenstein's laboratory; on the opposite side was an elegant table, chair, and easy chair in Clerval's house; while between the two there was a blank space. The scene changes were effected by lighting the house or the laboratory as was required, which allowed the actors two thirds of the acting area on which to perform. This arrangement made it possible for the scenes to flow into each other almost cinematically.

In the interval after Act One, the laboratory was cleared, leaving the space for the cellar. The centre area was used for the short scene in the prison, with both the house and the cellar in darkness.

ACT ONE

Scene One

THE LABORATORY

FRANKENSTEIN *is sitting at his bench. He is an earnest young man in his early twenties. He appears to be asleep. At first only his white face can be seen by the candlelight, but the clouds obscuring a full moon drift away, and the blue-green light of the night sky fills the room. It can then be seen that he is coatless, and the left sleeve of his shirt is rolled up to the shoulder. A crude tourniquet is tied around the upper part of his arm, and below it is a splash of dried blood.*

He stirs, and his lips move in a whisper. His right hand moves along the bench until it encounters a stoppered jar. He holds the jar up to the light.

FRANKENSTEIN: Fluid. (*With a sob of relief and exultation.*) Still fluid!

The movement draws his attention to his arm, which hangs useless by his side. He tears off the tourniquet. He winces, cries out, and slumps back into his seat again.

After a second or two there is a halloing outside, and a clatter on the stairs. CLERVAL *appears in the doorway, and peers into the room. He is about* FRANKENSTEIN'S *age. He tends to hide his feelings under a cloak of flippancy.*

CLERVAL: Hullo. Anyone at home? (*He sees the slumped figure.*) Angels and ministers! (*He bounds over to* FRANKENSTEIN, *and turns his face to the light.* FRANKENSTEIN *groans slightly.*) I suppose any sign of life is a mercy. (*He slaps* FRANKENSTEIN'S *hand.*) Rouse yourself. This is Clerval. Remember me? Henri Clerval. What d'you call this—a fit of the vapours? What do you keep in this chemist's collection?

He clinks among the bottles on the bench, finally selects one, and reads the label by candlelight. After a short prayer for safety, he unstoppers the bottle, and sniffs. It takes his breath away. While he chokes, he waves the stopper under FRANKENSTEIN's *nose.* FRANKENSTEIN *coughs.* CLERVAL *returns the stopper to the bottle.*

FRANKENSTEIN *stirs, and sits up.*

FRANKENSTEIN: Who? ... Who?

CLERVAL: Me.

FRANKENSTEIN: How—did you get here?

CLERVAL: Up the stairs. Pleasant riverside quarters you have—sweating steps, and grey slime. Suicide's Corner, my guide informed me.

FRANKENSTEIN: What are you doing here?

CLERVAL: What are *you* doing here? Adding to the reputation of the district? Have you recovered, or do you need another whiff of reviver?

FRANKENSTEIN: How did you find me?

CLERVAL: You *were* snugly hidden.

FRANKENSTEIN: Not as well as I hoped.

CLERVAL: Obviously you weren't at home in the fashionable quarter of the town, otherwise the first mention of your name would have disgorged you. So you must have been buried where your reputation hadn't reached. I merely had to describe you in half a dozen hell-holes before an apprentice cut-throat led me to this mouldering hulk. (*Looks at the wounded arm.*) Why did you do it?

FRANKENSTEIN: An experiment.

CLERVAL: Dangerous.

FRANKENSTEIN: Successful.

CLERVAL: If it had failed? Self-murder is a crime, you know.

FRANKENSTEIN: I keep a journal. Somewhere—some day—the work would have been carried on.

CLERVAL: I see.

FRANKENSTEIN: Do you?

CLERVAL: Rather I realise further questioning to be pointless. Are you strong enough to walk?

FRANKENSTEIN *tries to rise, but fails.*

CLERVAL: No. (*Takes a flask from his pocket.*) Try this. It was a pity to waste it on you while you were unconscious.

FRANKENSTEIN *drinks.*

FRANKENSTEIN: I should have recovered within an hour. A living body quickly adjusts the blood supply. (*He hands the flask back to* CLERVAL.)

CLERVAL: Your health. (*He drinks.*) I can give you five more minutes in which to recover. In the meantime, we must do something about this arm. It would frighten the ladies into fits. There is water in this place, I suppose— apart from the stuff trickling down the walls.

FRANKENSTEIN: I set a bowl by the bench.

CLERVAL: Capital. (*Takes the bowl to* FRANKENSTEIN, *and sponges the blood from his arm.*) While I play nurse, you invent a tale to explain yourself . . . Ye gods! Did you use a razor or a hatchet? . . . Yesterday you left your room without warning to maid or valet . . .

FRANKENSTEIN: Yesterday?

CLERVAL: Genius takes no account of time. You took neither money nor change of clothes. You vanished like a bubble. Pop! If I hadn't agreed to take charge, the town crier would have been called.

FRANKENSTEIN: I was missed?

CLERVAL: Today is Elizabeth's birthday.

FRANKENSTEIN: Elizabeth! Today, of course.

CLERVAL: Naturally a man on the threshold of eternity doesn't consider birthdays.

FRANKENSTEIN: I'm a fool. I should have . . . But I had the answer. I couldn't pause. Even for food or sleep, I couldn't pause.

CLERVAL: Obviously. But it was an ill-timed disappearance. On her birthday a girl expects something from her fiancé. Some token—a bouquet, even a kind word or two. But from you, nothing. Disconcerting. However, the celebration is in progress—trusting my powers of detection to produce the guest of honour . . . Well? . . . Your story?

FRANKENSTEIN: You won't believe me.

CLERVAL: I don't ask for credibility. Merely some explanation.

FRANKENSTEIN: I work here.

CLERVAL: Work? Isn't your income enough? Or have deserving causes eaten your entire estate?

FRANKENSTEIN: Research. I continued after I was forced to leave university.

CLERVAL: The eternal scholar? . . . You'd better not use this arm again for a day or two.

FRANKENSTEIN: I bought this house two years ago. I have worked here since. Alone.

CLERVAL: Who on earth has been dining with us, then? Who has been courting Elizabeth? Who has been the mainstay of half a dozen philanthropic committees? You must have a double.

FRANKENSTEIN: Whatever claims society made upon my days, my nights were still my own . . . You do have irritating eyebrows, Clerval. Are they permanently raised?

CLERVAL: A hidden laboratory. A double life. Secret research by the light of a guttering candle. I'm baffled. What research, for instance?

FRANKENSTEIN: The blood on my arm was dry. (*Indicating the bottle to* CLERVAL.) Now examine that.

CLERVAL: More blood?

FRANKENSTEIN: Taken at the same time as the smear on my arm, but still fluid. Uncongealed. Still living.

CLERVAL: Remarkable. If there is ever a market for bottled blood, you'll double your fortune.

FRANKENSTEIN: That is why I hide like a recluse.

CLERVAL: Afraid of losing a fortune?

FRANKENSTEIN: Afraid of the too-easy laugh.

CLERVAL: I'm sorry.

FRANKENSTEIN: I'm not offended . . . Tonight I crossed the threshold. The experiment succeeded. Tomorrow I begin the last experiment. When that succeeds, I can . . . I shall . . . (*Stands shakily.*)

CLERVAL: Steady. You have a coat here?

FRANKENSTEIN: Somewhere.

CLERVAL *hunts for, and eventually finds the coat.*

FRANKENSTEIN: Clerval, do you remember my father?

CLERVAL: Slightly.

FRANKENSTEIN: Only slightly. He died when I was sixteen. They hailed him as a philanthropist, too. He devoted his time, and his fortune to the poor and the wretched. The town would have erected a statue to his memory, but he dismissed the idea. He said that his only monument would be to live in the hearts of his fellow men . . . You remember him "slightly".

CLERVAL: It *was* ten years ago.

FRANKENSTEIN: In two generations he will be forgotten.

CLERVAL: Moral—make sure of your statue early. Your coat. I'll help.

FRANKENSTEIN: I am in full possession of my faculties now. (*He takes the coat, and puts it on, though the effort makes him wince.*) My father was right. A man's only guarantee of immortality is the memory he leaves behind. A block of stone never kept a memory fresh. Only deeds can do that. You remember Alexander. Caesar . . . (*Firmly.*) I will be remembered, too.

CLERVAL: How many men will you slaughter to achieve your immortality?

FRANKENSTEIN: None.

CLERVAL: It can't be done. History only remembers the villains. The benefactors are ignored.

FRANKENSTEIN: I shall be remembered as long as there are men in the world. Believe me, Clerval, in centuries to come my name will be whispered with awe.

CLERVAL: Victor, the guests are waiting. Elizabeth, too.

FRANKENSTEIN: My name will be my monument.

CLERVAL: Come along.

FRANKENSTEIN *goes with him to the door. There, he pauses and looks behind. He draws himself up proudly, and pronounces his name as though it were a challenge to posterity.*

FRANKENSTEIN: Frankenstein!

ACT ONE

Scene Two

CLERVAL'S HOUSE

The atmosphere here is of simple elegance in contrast with the sinister brooding of the laboratory.

ELIZABETH *stands alone at the window. In her early twenties, she is warm-hearted, but with a will of her own.*
JUSTINE *enters. She is a maidservant of* ELIZABETH'S *age.*

JUSTINE: Miss Elizabeth . . .

ELIZABETH: Justine?

JUSTINE: He's here. With M. Clerval.

ELIZABETH: Thank you . . . Have I—been missed in the music room?

JUSTINE: It wouldn't be right to say "no". But Master William's been reciting M. Clerval's poetry—all owls, and graves, and goings on at midnight. The company took it funnier than a raree show.

ELIZABETH: Isn't it past his bed-time?

JUSTINE: He's to be allowed up 'till after supper tonight. I'll see that he doesn't over-tire.

ELIZABETH: Death's heads and rattling bones are for the broad daylight. He mustn't have nightmares.

JUSTINE: I look after him, miss. Like—my own.

ELIZABETH: I know.

MME. COUPER, *a middle-aged self indulgent widow, gushes into the room.*

MME. COUPER: Elizabeth, my dear. Nothing fantastic and terrible I hope.

ELIZABETH: The room was hot, but I have recovered, thank you.

MME. COUPER: Frankenstein. What happened to your fiancé? Spirited away like a thing on Walpurgis Night.

ELIZABETH: He has returned. He is in the house now.

MME. COUPER: How disappointing! I mean, what an ordinary ending to an improbable adventure.

JUSTINE (*who disapproves strongly of* MME. COUPER): Supper will be ready directly, ma'am.

ELIZABETH: Thank you, Justine.

JUSTINE *curtseys and leaves the room.* MME. COUPER *eyes her coldly as she passes.*

MME. COUPER: Really, servants are impossible.

ELIZABETH: Justine?

MME. COUPER: She announced supper as though my mind dwelt on nothing but food. Presuming creature! I hear she was rescued by dear Baron Frankenstein. From the gutter, and a fate worse . . .

ELIZABETH: We are fond of Justine. She has been with us for five years.

MME. COUPER: But you all have such generous natures. Five years? It does give credibility to the rumours.

ELIZABETH: I never listen to scandal, unless I intend to spread it further.

MME. COUPER: Nor I. (*She considers what she has been led to admit, and her attitude towards* ELIZABETH *cools.*) The child is five years old, too. Strange.

ELIZABETH: No doubt gossip makes it stranger. Frankenstein's generosity . . .

MME. COUPER: Please continue. The Baron's philanthropy intrigues me.

ELIZABETH: I am an item of the Baron's philanthropy.

MME. COUPER: My dear Elizabeth!

ELIZABETH: I never knew my parents. I was scarcely out of the cradle when Frankenstein's father—rescued me. Everything I have, everything I am, I owe to Frankenstein and his father. If I live here in the Clerval house, it is because gossip forbids me to share Frankenstein's roof until we are married.

MME. COUPER: But, my dear, you *are* to marry him.

ELIZABETH: Would it have silenced the scandalmongers if Frankenstein had married Justine? . . . I am sure supper is quite ready now, Mme. Couper.

FRANKENSTEIN *appears in the doorway, his damaged arm in a sling.*

FRANKENSTEIN: Elizabeth.

ELIZABETH: Victor!

FRANKENSTEIN: Many happy returns, my dear.

ELIZABETH *crosses to him, alarmed by the sling.*

FRANKENSTEIN: Nothing but a scratch. No duels or swashbuckling. (*Lying unconvincingly.*) A jolt in the coach. A fragment of glass.

ELIZABETH: Where were you?

FRANKENSTEIN: Hurrying back to you.

He is about to kiss her when MME. COUPER *clears her throat.* FRANKENSTEIN *notices her for the first time.*

FRANKENSTEIN: Good evening.

MME. COUPER: Please don't restrain your emotions on my account. I shan't breathe a syllable.

CLERVAL *enters with his father.*

CLERVAL SENIOR *is a magistrate in late middle-age.*

MME. COUPER: Company! What a provoking world it is for lovers.

CLERVAL: Here's a fine quartet of hosts. Have we all deserted our guests?

ELIZABETH: I had an absurd premonition. But it was merely overheated fancy. Here is Frankenstein.

CLERVAL: Overheated? You must partner father here. He was casting a graveyard chill over the entire music room.

CLERVAL SNR.: One of the penalties of taking office as a magistrate. You carry the conscience of the city. But take no notice. Away and enjoy yourselves.

CLERVAL: And what is the incubus that weighs down my parent? A mere matter of body-snatching.

CLERVAL SNR.: It's no subject for joking.

FRANKENSTEIN: Body-snatching?

CLERVAL SNR.: I've just had news that young Lavin's coffin was broken open—a few hours after the funeral. A common thief I can understand. But a ghoul . . . A despoiler of graves . . .

CLERVAL: A frugal minded fellow who sees no harm in helping himself to something you have finished with. Once I'm dead, I shan't give a button for what happens to my remains. Of course, I'd prefer a more romantic end, but if I can be of service on a dissecting slab, let the doctors carve away.

MME. COUPER *shudders*.

FRANKENSTEIN: The grave robbers—who are they?

CLERVAL SNR.: We have our suspicions, but nothing can be proved. And responsible men baulk us.

CLERVAL: Lecturers at the medical school.

CLERVAL SNR.: Let one of the creatures be brought before me. He'll learn what the law is.

FRANKENSTEIN: The penalties are heavy?

CLERVAL SNR.: For trading in human flesh?

MME. COUPER: Ugh!

CLERVAL SNR.: I apologise, ma'am. The pup argues, and I ramble on. Let me take you in to supper.

MME. COUPER: I believe I've lost my appetite.

CLERVAL SNR.: Nonsense. Wait until you've sampled the pâté. Capital pâté. You'll come too, Frankenstein?

FRANKENSTEIN: With pleasure.

CLERVAL SENIOR *takes out* MME. COUPER.

ELIZABETH: You're still faint. The arm . . .

FRANKENSTEIN: Perfectly well.

ELIZABETH: You're pale . . . Are you coming, Clerval?

CLERVAL: Naturally . . . Frankenstein.

FRANKENSTEIN: Yes?

CLERVAL: I'm a very indifferent poet, I know; but any poet has an eye for the fantastic.

FRANKENSTEIN: What have you seen?

CLERVAL: You *are* pale. Do you share my father's concern for the resurrection men?

FRANKENSTEIN: I was wondering how far the lecturers were justified. If the wretches who supply their materials are caught—what then?

CLERVAL: A term of imprisonment. Perhaps a whipping. Are the lecturers justified?

FRANKENSTEIN: I still have to make up my mind.

CLERVAL: Be careful.

FRANKENSTEIN: What do you mean?

CLERVAL: Just—be careful—how you make up your mind. By the way, I have a nodding acquaintance with a student at the hospital. For the price of a bottle he might tell you a tale or so. No more than the police know, of course; but afterwards—you are used to thinking for yourself.

ELIZABETH: You must keep your whimsies within bounds, Clerval. Frankenstein is hardly likely to open graves.

CLERVAL: You should know what Frankenstein is capable of, my dear . . . Did someone mention supper?

FRANKENSTEIN: Come along.

He goes out with ELIZABETH.

CLERVAL: I'd like to know what you are capable of, dear friend. I'd like to know.

He follows them out.

ACT ONE

Scene Three

THE LABORATORY

FRANKENSTEIN enters the attic. He crosses to the bench and makes an entry in his journal.

FRANKENSTEIN: 21st September, 1817.

He examines a jar in which a shapeless piece of matter is floating, then gives a cry of disappointment.

In the distance a church clock strikes.

FRANKENSTEIN (*beating the bench with frustration*): Time. Time. Time!

ACT ONE

Scene Four

CLERVAL'S HOUSE

CLERVAL is reading to ELIZABETH.

CLERVAL:

"Sees shades on shades with deeper tint impend,
Till chill and damp the moonless night descend."

He looks up at ELIZABETH. ELIZABETH'S thoughts are far away.

CLERVAL (*a little louder*): Till chill and damp the moonless night descend.

There is still no reply from ELIZABETH.

CLERVAL: I wrote no more: that is the end.

ELIZABETH (*suddenly remembering where she is*): Oh?

CLERVAL: I might have contrived a further twenty verses, but inspiration expired with the heroine.

ELIZABETH: It was charming.

CLERVAL: "The night owl screams oe'r his victim's corse"? You didn't hear a word. You may as well confess. I forgive you in advance.

ELIZABETH: He wrote half a page a week ago.

CLERVAL: If you wanted a man with a literary turn of mind you should have promised yourself to me instead of Frankenstein. It's to be published, you know. On real paper with genuine ink, and bound in guaranteed leather. "The Collected Poems Of Henri Clerval". They'd have been dedicated to Frankenstein, only, in some strange way, he seemed to think that would place him in my debt. He can't bear to be indebted to anyone: the balance must be all the other way. It's a sort of spiritual usury . . . Sorry. You love him, don't you?

ELIZABETH: I'm sure of nothing any longer. Unless I hang upon his arm, he's not even sure that I'm near. In the last six months he has been away for four.

CLERVAL: Business.

ELIZABETH: And each time he returns haggard, wild-eyed, and further from me than ever. What business does that? Clerval, something is driving him to despair. And you have seen it, too. I'm afraid.

CLERVAL: For him?

ELIZABETH: A sheltered life brings its own problems. I know so little of the world outside.

CLERVAL: Nonsense. You're as up-to-date as I am.

ELIZABETH: There is no horror like the unknown.

CLERVAL: He is doing nothing that could possibly touch you. Harmless bees buzzing in his bonnet.

ELIZABETH: You promise that?

CLERVAL: Word of honour.

ELIZABETH: Then you do know what he is doing.

CLERVAL: Well—in a remote, uncomprehending fashion.

ELIZABETH: And where he is.

CLERVAL: Rome? Paris? Berlin?

ELIZABETH: He is not in Rome, Paris, or Berlin.

CLERVAL: Oh, if you know better than I do . . .

ELIZABETH: Clerval!

CLERVAL: I make no more suggestions.

ELIZABETH: Go to him.

CLERVAL: He may be at the end of the earth.

ELIZABETH: For my sake.

CLERVAL: Feminine wiles from you, Elizabeth? I'm disappointed. I thought you were a rational creature.

ELIZABETH: All the more reason to believe me when I tell you that I feel death in the air.

CLERVAL makes a gesture of helplessness.

ELIZABETH: We grew up together. We shared our secrets. When he was happy, I was happy. When he despaired, I felt that the end of the world was near . . . Either bring him to me, Clerval, or take me to him.

CLERVAL: You're a confounded nuisance, Elizabeth . . . I'll do it. I'll end with thanks from neither of you, but I'll do it.

ELIZABETH: Bless you.

CLERVAL: I'm fond of you, too, Elizabeth. In a brotherly way. But don't expect miracles.

He goes out.

ELIZABETH *watches him go, then hurries to the door.*

ELIZABETH: Justine! Justine, bring my cloak.

She goes out.

ACT ONE

Scene Five

THE LABORATORY

FRANKENSTEIN *rubs his eyes, picks up a pen, and begins to write.*

FRANKENSTEIN: Experiment begun September 21st, 1817 ... Failed.

He hears a slight sound, and his whole attitude immediately changes. He sits up stiffly. He gets up from the bench, and crosses to the doorway.

FRANKENSTEIN: I warn you, I'm armed. A false step, and I'll fire. Raise your arms and come into the light.

Arms raised and whistling CLERVAL *comes into the attic.*

CLERVAL: Aren't we rather grown-up to be playing at soldiers?

FRANKENSTEIN: Clerval!

CLERVAL: Don't shoot. I surrender.

FRANKENSTEIN: What are you doing here?

CLERVAL: Manners, my dear fellow. The correct enquiry is "how do you do?" By the way, how *do* you do? When did you last sleep, for instance?

FRANKENSTEIN: Last night. The night before. A week ago. Since when have you been so interested in my health?

CLERVAL: Since you lost interest in it yourself. Elizabeth is worried, too. Do you remember Elizabeth?

FRANKENSTEIN: Days pass when I hardly remember my own name. Nothing exists but the work in front of me.

CLERVAL: Six months ago I understood the work was nearly finished.

FRANKENSTEIN: Six months ago. Since then the end has been in sight—always in sight—and always just beyond my reach.

CLERVAL: May one who has been burning with curiosity for six months ask what this work may be?

FRANKENSTEIN: No.

CLERVAL: I apologise.

FRANKENSTEIN: I sound like a boor. One forgets social graces in these surroundings. I meant that I couldn't ask anyone to share the risk until the work is completed.

CLERVAL: Risk? What a witch's kitchen. Incidentally, you should be dining with us tonight. Don't delay me by quibbling. I don't relish the thought of lingering here. The place is like a charnel house. Where do you keep the corpses?

FRANKENSTEIN: Where . . .?

CLERVAL: My sense of humour. The big fellow on the bench outside. The thing covered by a sheet.

FRANKENSTEIN: You didn't touch it?

CLERVAL: Bless you, no. It didn't strike my fancy. Looked for all the world like an undertaker's customer. Oh, I stumbled over another piece of apparatus at the bottom of the stairs. It must have made the noise that disturbed you.

FRANKENSTEIN: What—apparatus?

CLERVAL (*walking to the door*): A spade. (*Suddenly he*

stops and returns to FRANKENSTEIN.) Would you object strongly if I didn't leave immediately?

FRANKENSTEIN: You must.

CLERVAL: A ray just penetrated this block.

FRANKENSTEIN: Go at once. Never think of this place again.

CLERVAL: You're in danger, dear fellow. You aren't aware how much.

FRANKENSTEIN: Everything I have done has been calculated. The risk as carefully as the blood-flow of . . .

CLERVAL: Of?

FRANKENSTEIN: Leave me.

CLERVAL: I'm trying to help you.

FRANKENSTEIN: I have never asked for any man's help.

CLERVAL: Then it's time you did.

FRANKENSTEIN: As carefully as the blood-flow of a rat.

CLERVAL: Rat?

FRANKENSTEIN: Rat.

CLERVAL: Thank heavens for that. It's a small step from stealing a corpse to creating one. Our lives hang by such slender threads: a grain of poison, a twist of rope, and we are no more than subjects for the dissecting room.

FRANKENSTEIN: What are you trying to make me admit?

CLERVAL: It was a new spade. You've only recently taken to digging for your own specimens.

FRANKENSTEIN: If I allowed you one scrap of evidence, it would make you an accessory. Will you go before it is too late?

CLERVAL: You confine yourself too closely here. You should take a constitutional more often. Hear the news. But who am I to blame you? I hear it, and it means nothing to me . . . A resurrection man was arrested a month ago. He is to be executed next week.

FRANKENSTEIN: He couldn't be guillotined for opening a grave.

CLERVAL: He was an Italian, he said. But like so much of his defence, there was no proof.

FRANKENSTEIN: You know police procedure. That isn't a capital crime.

CLERVAL: He refused to give details of his client. Even though the police tried to persuade him. He had an unexpected sense of loyalty. Quite unsuspected in such a low type.

FRANKENSTEIN: He mustn't die.

CLERVAL: Don't fret. It's a quick death. One clean cut and finis. He was a murderer. Several times over. He confessed eventually to that.

FRANKENSTEIN: A murderer!

CLERVAL: As I said—a very small step. Only one of his victims was found. The last. The others had disappeared.

In silence FRANKENSTEIN *walks to the bench. He sits, heavily, and covers his face with his hands.*

CLERVAL: I wish Elizabeth hadn't made me come tonight.

FRANKENSTEIN: Murdered! They were murdered.

CLERVAL: I say too much.

FRANKENSTEIN: I'm to blame.

CLERVAL: Only for your ignorance. The rest was his responsibility.

FRANKENSTEIN: My responsibility. I wouldn't have it otherwise. The only question—was it justified? It must be justified. It must. Now more than ever. If only for their sakes. If they died for nothing . . . The work must be completed.

CLERVAL: I know nothing about—the work.

There is a pause. FRANKENSTEIN *paces the room, then turns to* CLERVAL.

FRANKENSTEIN: You know half the story. The black half. It's only right now that you should know the rest.

CLERVAL: If you're quite sure . . .

FRANKENSTEIN: Only the whole truth now could make it bearable. But, believe me, Clerval, I knew nothing of the murders. You must believe that.

CLERVAL: My dear fellow, you're the gentlest creature alive.

FRANKENSTEIN: And you must swear never to repeat to a living soul what I tell you.

CLERVAL: Ought we to seal the compact in blood?

FRANKENSTEIN: This is desperately serious.

CLERVAL: My lightest word is serious.

FRANKENSTEIN: Did you ever hear why I left the university?

CLERVAL: I presumed it had no more to offer.

FRANKENSTEIN: I was—asked to leave. You see, to the learned professors, I was a fool, a heretic, an offence. All my work since has been undertaken in secret.

CLERVAL: Ah!

FRANKENSTEIN: And it is almost complete . . . Clerval . . .

CLERVAL: Yes?

FRANKENSTEIN: I have unravelled the secret of life.

CLERVAL: A fair enough proposition. What does it mean?

FRANKENSTEIN: I could make a dead man walk again.

CLERVAL: If I swallow hard, it doesn't entirely mean that I disbelieve you.

FRANKENSTEIN: I hardly expect you to believe. They wouldn't—the men of learning: the men who know everything.

CLERVAL: You do seem to claim supernatural powers.

FRANKENSTEIN: Everything we don't understand is supernatural. To a savage, the sun is a god; a tinder-box a miracle.

CLERVAL: You have—proof, of course.

FRANKENSTEIN: For myself—yes. The final proof would be the raising of a dead man.

CLERVAL: Then produce your proof, and confound the professors.

FRANKENSTEIN: Me? Discredited? If I made the offer, I should be hustled into a strait-jacket. If I restore the man in secret, the doctors will deny that he ever died. I know the world as well as you, Clerval.

CLERVAL: A problem.

FRANKENSTEIN: I have solved it.

CLERVAL: How?

FRANKENSTEIN: I have created a man. He will be my proof. When he walks, no one will be able to deny me. I shall have brought to the world the greatest gift since the discovery of fire. I shall have conquered the last enemy.

CLERVAL: Pardon my doubts—you created a man?

FRANKENSTEIN: Muscle, bone, and nerve. You saw him out there.

CLERVAL: That monster? Men don't grow to those dimensions.

FRANKENSTEIN: Then he will be more than a man. It will take more than a man to shatter the convictions of centuries. He will have the strength of ten men. And he will be a mere beginning. That will be my proof. There will be no doubts then. I shall see the dawn of a new age.

CLERVAL: An ecstatic prospect. When does it begin?

FRANKENSTEIN: I was ready six months ago. But there have been delays. And each delay breeds more delay. A hot summer, and an oppressive autumn.

CLERVAL: Decay?

FRANKENSTEIN: Leaves wither, and the apples rot where they fall . . . There is only one thing needful, but I must have it soon. Before the rest begins to decompose again. If it does, the work must be started afresh. A treadmill. Six months already. It may be six years.

CLERVAL: The one thing needful?

FRANKENSTEIN: A brain.

CLERVAL: Why should that delay you? Half my friends manage without.

FRANKENSTEIN: He must have a mind to match his body. Strong and resourceful. I tried surgery on the materials I have, but my skill is limited.

CLERVAL: A mere brain.

FRANKENSTEIN: The brain of a man in the prime of life—healthy and vigorous.

CLERVAL: Very few men are likely to part with their heads—even in the interests of science. The ones who do are unwilling.

FRANKENSTEIN: The ones who do?

CLERVAL: It happens now and again.

FRANKENSTEIN: Such men exist? Where?

CLERVAL: Your grave-digging friend, for instance. By this time next week, he will . . .

CLERVAL'S *voice dies away. He and* FRANKENSTEIN *stare at each other.*

FRANKENSTEIN: How—does one gain admittance to the prison?

ACT ONE

Scene Six

THE LABORATORY

FRANKENSTEIN *stands triumphantly in the centre of the attic, by the body which lies covered by a sheet on an operating trolly.*

FRANKENSTEIN: It is complete.

CLERVAL *is slumped over the bench. He raises his head.*

CLERVAL (*pulling himself together*): The execution unnerved me. I never saw a man die violently before.

FRANKENSTEIN: Will you stay to the end?

CLERVAL: I must. (*With an attempt to laugh lightly.*) I feel cheated when I wake in the middle of a nightmare. My hair stands on end, but I must learn what was lurking in the shadows. When will you begin the last process?

FRANKENSTEIN: Tonight.

CLERVAL: So soon?

FRANKENSTEIN: It must be.

CLERVAL: Look. My hands. Fluttering like leaves.

FRANKENSTEIN: The delicate operation was over an hour ago. I worked in a trance.

CLERVAL: But tonight!

FRANKENSTEIN: Have you seen the clouds?

CLERVAL: They don't inspire me.

FRANKENSTEIN: The high clouds move towards us; the low clouds fly from us. Cross winds. Within the hour we shall be in the centre of the storm.

CLERVAL: Is that vital?

FRANKENSTEIN: The atmosphere is charged with electricity. I shall direct it through the mass lying there. Unless I have pursued a mirage, I shall have my final proof. Cornelius Agrippa, Paracelsus, Albertus Magnus: they died searching for the elixir of life. It was before them all the time—flaming in the sky.

CLERVAL: The oak doesn't welcome a thunderbolt.

FRANKENSTEIN: There are poisons here—strychnine, arsenic, cyanide—any one of them could strike you dead. But a physician knows how to use them. I've no intention of exposing my handiwork to an uncontrolled blast. But, when the lightning strikes, I shall know how to direct it.

CLERVAL: When it strikes?

FRANKENSTEIN: There is a conducting apparatus on the roof. It attracts the charge towards us. You can operate that. It needs nothing but brute strength.

CLERVAL: So right for me. But you?

FRANKENSTEIN: Co-ordinate the reactions of the body. Simulate breathing and heartbeats until the living machinery works for itself.

CLERVAL: And then?

FRANKENSTEIN: We hope.

CLERVAL: It's not too late, even now.

FRANKENSTEIN: Too late?

CLERVAL: To turn back. Give that unborn thing a decent burial. Lock the door, and leave the house to the storm.

FRANKENSTEIN: I have nursed this dream since I was a child. Turn back now?

CLERVAL: The experiment may fail. There is more to a man than a body.

FRANKENSTEIN: A failure can be destroyed, another experiment begun ... Hark. Did you hear that?

CLERVAL: Hear?

FRANKENSTEIN: Thunder in the mountains. The storm is blowing this way. There's no time to lose. Quickly. This rod clamps to the end of the charging table. Hurry. There is a connecting plate at the head of the table, and another at the foot: the force will flow between the two. It is discharged through another rod ... There. Did you hear that?

CLERVAL: The wind around the rooftops, and a door banging below.

FRANKENSTEIN: A drum-roll among the peaks. All the might of nature heralding a new life!

CLERVAL: A door.

FRANKENSTEIN: A door?

CLERVAL: Banging below.

FRANKENSTEIN: But ...

He looks towards the doorway. ELIZABETH *stands there.*
FRANKENSTEIN: Elizabeth!

ELIZABETH: Victor? I have been following Clerval. I have been spying. Now I have shame to add to my other emotions. I am not invited in. Am I so unwelcome?

FRANKENSTEIN (*still dazed*): You should never have come.

CLERVAL (*covering Frankenstein's too brutal remark*): This is no quarter for you, Elizabeth. Positively dangerous. How far did you walk unattended?

ELIZABETH: I passed other women in the street. They were unattended.

CLERVAL: This is neither the time nor the place to explain them. Come with me, Elizabeth. I'll take you home.

ELIZABETH: No, Clerval. I spent all my courage in coming. I may never summon up so much again.

FRANKENSTEIN: The storm will break at any minute.

ELIZABETH: And there is no shelter for me here?

CLERVAL: Elizabeth, my dear . . .

ELIZABETH: Leave us, Clerval.

CLERVAL: Together? Here?

ELIZABETH: As you said, this is neither the time nor the place. But we are together. Here and now. Leave us.

CLERVAL: Frankenstein . . .

FRANKENSTEIN (*in control again*): Be within call.

CLERVAL: Be gentle with each other.

He goes out.

ELIZABETH: This is Rome—Paris—Berlin?

FRANKENSTIN: I deceived you.

ELIZABETH: No. I didn't believe you . . . But—I—didn't expect this either. I'm—confused.

FRANKENSTEIN: Would you rather have found me opium-drugged among the ruins of an orgy?

ELIZABETH: I should understand your reasons then . . . All I know now is that you never trusted me.

FRANKENSTEIN: Did you trust me?

ELIZABETH: This is a cold moment. Suddenly we are strangers.

A low rumble of thunder is heard. FRANKENSTEIN *half-turns towards the window.*

ELIZABETH: You wish I were gone.

FRANKENSTEIN: I . . .

ELIZABETH: Your voice says so. Your eyes say so. Can your words contradict them?

FRANKENSTEIN: If I could explain . . .

ELIZABETH: Is that impossible?

FRANKENSTEIN: Yes.

ELIZABETH: Because I am a stranger?

FRANKENSTEIN: Because you are a woman.

ELIZABETH: Never let that be your excuse. A woman is neither angel nor devil. She is a human being. I was born with a heart and a brain. I can feel and understand . . . There are lines in your face that I never saw before.

FRANKENSTEIN: I grow older.

ELIZABETH: And this house is so full of shadows.

FRANKENSTEIN: Your place is in the light.

ELIZABETH: My place is with you.

Another rumble of thunder.

FRANKENSTEIN: Why did you come here?

ELIZABETH: To help you.

FRANKENSTEIN: Oh, my dear Elizabeth . . .

ELIZABETH: A dry laugh. Is that all my help is worth?

Another rumble of thunder.

ELIZABETH: Your hands are trembling. What are you hiding from me?

FRANKENSTEIN: Nothing.

ELIZABETH: You make me feel useless and foolish.

FRANKENSTEIN: You have been a little absurd, my dear.

ELIZABETH breaks away from him.

ELIZABETH: Next year we are to be married. Will our life together never be more than this?

FRANKENSTEIN: This?

ELIZABETH: Hands touching in the half-light. Thoughts hidden. Why did you agree to marry me?

FRANKENSTEIN: Because I love you.

ELIZABETH: Love embraces more than you imagine. What does it mean to you?

FRANKENSTEIN: I cherish you, care for you, keep you from harm.

ELIZABETH: You could do as much for a caged linnet. What will there be for *me* to do?

FRANKENSTEIN: You will love me in return.

ELIZABETH: Singing for you after supper? Can't you understand? I want to share your life.

FRANKENSTEIN: So you shall. To the last crust.

ELIZABETH: The last blow, and heartache, too?

FRANKENSTEIN: If you insist.

ELIZABETH: Why did you never mention this place?

FRANKENSTEIN: Because, for you, it could never exist.

ELIZABETH: It does exist. I can stand between its slimy walls. I can smell the river slithering by. I can feel the shapeless thing under this cover.

FRANKENSTEIN: For God's sake, don't touch that!

He knocks her arm away. There is a pause as they face each other, neither knowing how to speak again after the moment of violence.

ELIZABETH: It was wrong of me to come.

FRANKENSTEIN: I didn't—hurt you?

ELIZABETH: Only a little. I should have been prepared.

She walks to the door.

ELIZABETH: Can a promise bind strangers? I must release you from yours, Victor. Don't be distressed. You will find the woods full of linnets.

She goes out.

FRANKENSTEIN: Elizabeth. (*He runs to the doorway, calling after her.*) Elizabeth!

As he reaches the doorway, the room is lit by a vivid flash of lightning. He stops and turns to stare at the thing lying amongst the apparatus. There is a clap of thunder.

FRANKENSTEIN (*whispering*): Elizabeth.

Dreamily he walks over to the apparatus. CLERVAL *hurries into the room.*

CLERVAL: What have you done to Elizabeth? An avenging angel rushed past me on the stairs.

FRANKENSTEIN: Gone?

CLERVAL: Out of the house, slamming the door to the tune of that crack of doom.

FRANKENSTEIN: Gone.

CLERVAL: Don't you intend to follow?

FRANKENSTEIN: The storm is breaking. We must stay. This is the moment, Clerval. (*He adjusts various pieces of mechanism.*)

CLERVAL: Oh, why must I be pulled in two directions at once?

Lightning.

FRANKENSTEIN: A chance passes with every flash of lightning.

CLERVAL goes to the flywheel, and turns it.

CLERVAL: It's heavy.

FRANKENSTEIN: The faster you turn, the lighter it becomes.

Throughout the storm each man works in his own way.

The lightning is repeated at shorter and shorter intervals, until the thunder becomes an almost continuous roll.

FRANKENSTEIN: Turn. Turn.

CLERVAL: It hums.

FRANKENSTEIN: It throbs. It pounds. The force is rushing through.

CLERVAL: My hands itch and tingle.

FRANKENSTEIN: Sparks are leaping between the points. The air is vibrating with life.

CLERVAL: That flash was near.

FRANKENSTEIN: Turn. Turn. Slowly. Slowly. The lungs are expanding. The heart is beating. The sluggish blood begins to flow. The cold clay warms.

Finally there is a flash like the crack of a whip, followed immediately by a deafening crash, and the falling of bricks.

CLERVAL: Struck!

FRANKENSTEIN: Turn.

But there is now no response to his manipulation. He gives a cry of dismay.

FRANKENSTEIN: Oh, no! Look.

CLERVAL: The moment of revelation?

FRANKENSTEIN: Dead. Dead. The controls are dead.

CLERVAL: That last flash. What damage?

FRANKENSTEIN: Fool that I am, I thought I could master any force.

CLERVAL: Serious?

FRANKENSTEIN: I should have tested, and tested. To fail now . . .

CLERVAL: The cannonade is passing.

FRANKENSTEIN: At the last stroke to fail!

CLERVAL: Who says we failed. The patient?

He puts his hand on the cover, but immediately gives a cry, and is hurled to the ground.

FRANKENSTEIN: Clerval!

He hurries to Clerval, who lies without moving.

FRANKENSTEIN: Clerval. Hurt?

CLERVAL *moans, and stirs.*

FRANKENSTEIN: What happened?

He helps CLERVAL *to his feet.* CLERVAL's *arm hangs limply.*

CLERVAL: My arm.

FRANKENSTEIN: The shock.

CLERVAL: Give me a minute. I assume the coloured lights and church bells only exist in my imagination.

FRANKENSTEIN: Your hand.

CLERVAL: A mere scorch. To remind us what happens to children who play with fire.

FRANKENSTEIN: You need . . .

CLERVAL: Brandy. But we lack the refinements of civilisation here. Don't worry. Life is returning. I almost wish it weren't. It feels as though an army of witches were sticking pins into me. There. I can move my fingers again.

FRANKENSTEIN: You frightened me.

CLERVAL: I misunderstood you. I thought you explained that the charge was drained away.

FRANKENSTEIN: It should have been. I . . . (*He kneels at the base of the apparatus.*)

CLERVAL: The answer?

FRANKENSTEIN: I was about to couple this rod when Elizabeth . . . (*He stands, slowly.*) I failed before I began.

CLERVAL: There'll be another storm. This is the season. Tomorrow or the next day.

FRANKENSTEIN: I failed.

CLERVAL: Listen. Here comes the rain.

FRANKENSTEIN: I deserve every scornful laugh I ever heard.

CLERVAL: Gentle, soothing rain. Like tears.

FRANKENSTEIN: I had immortality in my grasp, and I let it go. Fool. Fool.

CLERVAL: We're all human.

FRANKENSTEIN: What excuse is that?

CLERVAL: Come away with me now.

FRANKENSTEIN: Why?

CLERVAL: One doesn't linger on a battlefield. It harbours too many ghosts. There's no comfort for you amongst this debris. Besides, you've forgotten what warm food and clean sheets are like. When you've rested, you'll be ready to forgive yourself.

FRANKENSTEIN: I must stay.

CLERVAL: What can you do besides brood over your shortcomings?

FRANKENSTEIN: The journal must be completed—mistakes and all.

CLERVAL: There'll be twenty-four hours in tomorrow. Why not sleep until then?

FRANKENSTEIN: I must keep the record while the details are fresh.

CLERVAL: Don't you trust your memory?

FRANKENSTEIN: I trusted it tonight. I need to be alone, Clerval.

CLERVAL: With him? The unborn?

FRANKENSTEIN: He'll live yet.

He sits at the bench, and picks up a pen.

CLERVAL watches him irresolutely.

CLERVAL: It would be useless to argue, wouldn't it? Besides, one of us must follow Elizabeth. But, if I leave, promise that there will be no more experiments tonight.

FRANKENSTEIN: I promise.

CLERVAL: I shall tell Elizabeth that you are following shortly after me.

He goes out. After a short pause the door bangs. At the sound, FRANKENSTEIN seems to lose most of his self possession. He covers his face with his hands, and gives a sob. He gets up, and goes over to the body. He is about to turn back the cover, but changes his mind. He shrugs his shoulders, and his arms drop helplessly. He returns slowly to the bench, sits, and picks up his pen.

FRANKENSTEIN: "Experiment begun 12th October, 1817. Time—9.45..."

He writes. Soon he becomes absorbed in his work. For some time there is stillness in the room, only broken by the movement of his arm, and the scratching of his pen.

Then there is a movement under the sheet. The sheet rises and falls as though whatever is underneath is taking a deep breath. Then, very slowly, the thing rises to a sitting position. It pulls away the sheet which is covering its head, and stiffly looks from side to side. Except for its patchwork features, and huge stature, it might be a child waking in strange surroundings.

It slides from the table, and, after a slight uncertainty in maintaining its balance, stands erect.

FRANKENSTEIN hears the slight noise, and stops writing.

FRANKENSTEIN: Clerval?

He puts down his pen, and turns. After the first shock he stands, and takes a few steps towards THE CREATURE. THE CREATURE, hearing the noise behind it, turns to face FRANKENSTEIN. For a few seconds they stare at each other. Then THE CREATURE smiles, and raises its arm.

FRANKENSTEIN is horrified. He backs as THE CREATURE shuffles towards him, until he reaches the bench. There he is trapped until THE CREATURE'S outstretched hand touches his face. Then, with a cry, he faints.

CURTAIN

ACT TWO

Scene One

CLERVAL'S HOUSE

FRANKENSTEIN is sleeping in a large easy chair. He begins to pant and whimper. He leaps from the chair with a wild cry, then falls to his knees, covering his face with his hands.

ELIZABETH runs in to him.

ELIZABETH: Victor!

He takes his hands from his face, and looks up, bewildered. She assists him to his feet. He looks frantically *around the room for something which is not there, then turns to* ELIZABETH *again.*

FRANKENSTEIN: Elizabeth!

She takes his hands in hers.

ELIZABETH: You seemed asleep when I left you.

FRANKENSTEIN: I thought I saw . . . It grinned and gibbered . . . A nightmare. Only a nightmare. Over now.

ELIZABETH: Even the doctor was afraid for you.

FRANKENSTEIN: Doctor?

ELIZABETH: Clerval would hardly let him from the house until you were out of danger.

FRANKENSTEIN: That's absurd. I . . .

ELIZABETH: You have been very sick.

FRANKENSTEIN: Nonsense. A slight weakness, perhaps. Overwork . . .

ELIZABETH: You are still sick.

FRANKENSTEIN: My head—spins a little. My legs protest somewhat. Nothing that rest won't cure.

ELIZABETH: The doctor . . .

FRANKENSTEIN: If the doctor said differently, the doctor is a fool.

ELIZABETH: I nursed you.

FRANKENSTEIN (*apologetically*): Poor Elizabeth. Did I bark?

ELIZABETH: It's usual.

FRANKENSTEIN: For me?

ELIZABETH: When people cannot understand each other, they shout.

FRANKENSTEIN: How cold, starched, and efficient you've become. Have I offended you very deeply?

ELIZABETH: Not offended. The word is not "offended".

FRANKENSTEIN: How? My memory has become a patchwork thing.

ELIZABETH: Don't think. Don't try to think. Rest.

FRANKENSTEIN: My dear, I'm not dying. I may be in no condition for prize-fighting, but I'm master of my own body. Just give me time to recover my senses. You can still play nurse if you wish. Only—I can't remember—what happened—yesterday.

ELIZABETH *seats him in the chair again, and lightly massages his forehead.*

ELIZABETH: Close your eyes.

FRANKENSTEIN: How did I come to be here? I was—I was ... (*Gives a slight cry.*)

ELIZABETH: Hush now.

FRANKENSTEIN: The twinge of an old wound. We quarrelled. The storm. The—experiment. The failure. And then ... Then?

ELIZABETH: You were found senseless in the open street. The rain brought on a fever.

FRANKENSTEIN: And Clerval ...

ELIZABETH: He led a search for you.

FRANKENSTEIN: No ... After Clerval ... (*Gives a loud cry.*)

ELIZABETH: Victor!

FRANKENSTEIN: Clerval! (*Struggles to his feet.*) Where is Clerval?

ELIZABETH: In the house.

FRANKENSTEIN: Clerval. Clerval! (*He collapses into his chair.*) Oh, this damned weakness.

ELIZABETH (*To the door, and calling*): Clerval! (*To* FRANKENSTEIN.) Must you be so savage with yourself?

FRANKENSTEIN: Me—savage? Time and space are the enemies.

ELIZABETH: You are your own worst enemy.

FRANKENSTEIN: Space holds us prisoner while time murders us. Annihilate time and space, and men will be gods ... Oh, there's a death's-head chattering inside my skull.

CLERVAL *hurries in. He is holding a soldier doll.*

CLERVAL: Awake so soon?

FRANKENSTEIN: Clerval!

CLERVAL: Sitting up and shouting.

FRANKENSTEIN: Did you go back?

CLERVAL: Elizabeth, your patient is fretful. Remember the doctor's orders. Rest and quiet.

FRANKENSTEIN: Clerval.

CLERVAL: Go back? Where?

FRANKENSTEIN: To the house.

CLERVAL: I thought it best.

FRANKENSTEIN: What did you find?

CLERVAL: Nothing.

FRANKENSTEIN: Nothing?

CLERVAL: Except the rats, of course. They were having a fine time in the cellars. I could hear them dancing.

FRANKENSTEIN: Everything was as you saw it last?

CLERVAL: I didn't investigate the cellars too closely. Black as pitch, and rambling as a warren. Besides, I suppose you'd prefer the cellars to carry their own secrets.

ELIZABETH: Secrets?

CLERVAL: Elizabeth, my dear, would you consider me an ogre if I asked you to leave me with Frankenstein?

ELIZABETH: He should rest.

CLERVAL: He will once I've put his mind at ease. Unfortunately, I can't do that—um—in public.

FRANKENSTEIN: My dream was compounded of fear and hope. Once it is broken, there will be nothing to fear—and nothing to hope for.

CLERVAL: Elizabeth.

ELIZABETH: I trust you.

CLERVAL: Thank you. The patient will return docile to your ministrations.

ELIZABETH: Victor ...

FRANKENSTEIN: Here, Elizabeth. The man you always knew. A lesser man than I thought you knew.

ELIZABETH *goes out.*

CLERVAL (*dancing the doll as he watches her go*): Do you like the poppet? An English soldier—black hat, red coat, and all. For Young William. He was promised a good something if he would play quietly without disturbing you. He deserves it. You'd never realise there was a child in the house. (*He takes in* FRANKENSTEIN's *exasperated silence.*) I locked and bolted the ruin before I surrendered it to the rats. It would never have done to leave that house open for night prowlers. I take it you buried the remains in the cellar?

FRANKENSTEIN: Remains?

CLERVAL: The unsuccessful experiment.

FRANKENSTEIN: That was untouched. I couldn't even bring myself to uncover it. I only dreamed ...

CLERVAL: Then where ...?

FRANKENSTEIN: Where?

CLERVAL: Where did it go?

FRANKENSTEIN: It was left among the apparatus.

CLERVAL: You accomplished more in your delirium than you imagine. The laboratory was empty.

FRANKENSTEIN: Then . . .

CLERVAL: It could hardly have walked.

FRANKENSTEIN (*in an ecstatic whisper*): He put out his arms.

CLERVAL: The experiment failed. I was there. Remember?

FRANKENSTEIN (*with a triumphant cry*): Justified! Fool that I was to doubt for a second. I was justified.

CLERVAL: You were dreaming. If that monstrosity were alive, it would be loose. Do you think it could wander unnoticed around the town?

FRANKENSTEIN: You locked the house.

CLERVAL: I searched the rooms.

FRANKENSTEIN: Not the cellars.

CLERVAL: Why the cellars?

FRANKENSTEIN: Eyes that are used to darkness avoid the light.

CLERVAL: Poor devil, if it were.

FRANKENSTEIN: Why?

CLERVAL: Locked among the rats without food and water.

FRANKENSTEIN: How long?

CLERVAL: Since you were taken ill.

FRANKENSTEIN: How many hours?

CLERVAL: How many days. Over a week.

FRANKENSTEIN: A week? . . . I want bread. Immediately . . . The devil take this body of mine—every dram of strength is drained out of it ... Meat and wine ... If he should have died ... Let me stand, Clerval.

He tries to stand, but has to struggle against his own weakness, and CLERVAL's *attentions.*

CLERVAL: You're in no condition.

FRANKENSTEIN: I'm in no condition to do anything but struggle to that cellar. On my hands and knees if I must. A week!

CLERVAL: It put out its arms, you said.

FRANKENSTEIN: Did I? Then it must have done.

CLERVAL: The fear of it unhinged your mind. Dare you face it again?

FRANKENSTEIN: My creation? Dare I not face it again!

CLERVAL: At least listen to reason.

FRANKENSTEIN: Reason? Reason is a liar. In future only believe me when I talk of dreams. Reason tells me that I am feeble. In my heart I am at the house already. Are you with me? Then open these doors, and make way ...

With a tremendous effort, he gets up, pushes CLERVAL *out of the way, and strides to the door.*

ACT TWO

Scene Two

THE CELLAR

The cellar is in darkness, Enter CLERVAL *and* FRANKENSTEIN. FRANKENSTEIN *holds a lamp in one hand, and a cane in the other.*

ACT TWO

CLERVAL *is still clutching the doll from the previous scene.*

CLERVAL (*nervously*): Not so fast.

FRANKENSTEIN: You saw him.

CLERVAL: I saw it. That creature belongs to an old wives' tale—winter nights and chimney corners.

FRANKENSTEIN: I gave him life.

CLERVAL *takes the hand of* FRANKENSTEIN *which holds the lamp, and lifts it so that the light falls on* FRANKENSTEIN'S *face.*

CLERVAL: Your eyes are feverish. There's a strange light burning in them.

FRANKENSTEIN: The light of victory. Pride.

CLERVAL: Pride? That's a killing disease.

FRANKENSTEIN: I have dreamed dreams, and seen visions. I did more—I gave them life. You saw. You are convinced.

CLERVAL: I am convinced of the creature's strength. Its other virtues wait to be proved. (*Takes a flask from his pocket, and drinks.*) It would have torn me to pieces if you hadn't stopped it.

FRANKENSTEIN: He'd been locked up, starving, for days.

CLERVAL: We all have to learn self-control. You saw what it had done to the laboratory—that tangle of iron was once apparatus.

FRANKENSTEIN: You despise his strength.

CLERVAL: Despise? I'm afraid of it.

FRANKENSTEIN: There's nothing lacking that makes up a man.

CLERVAL: Where did you slip in the soul? You provided a heart: can it hold understanding, or is it a mere machine for pumping blood? . . . What was that?

FRANKENSTEIN: That?

CLERVAL: Scuffling beyond the shadows.

FRANKENSTEIN: The rats. The river? Who knows? . . . He is asleep.

CLERVAL: It eats. It drinks. It sleeps.

FRANKENSTEIN: A man.

CLERVAL (*dancing the doll*): Two arms. Two legs. A head. A man?

FRANKENSTEIN (*smiling*): Idiot. Why bring that with you?

CLERVAL: I fancy you dragged me from the house before I had time to part with it. I'm glad I brought him, though. Reassuring. Just now I should like to meditate on coal fires and muddy boots, boiled potatoes, and suet puddings. Familiar things . . . Down here we hardly belong to the world at all: Listen!

FRANKENSTEIN: He drank enough to put him to sleep for hours.

CLERVAL: What are you going to do with—him—out there?

FRANKENSTEIN: Use him.

CLERVAL: How?

FRANKENSTEIN: To convince the fools in authority that I was right. They tried to dismiss me as a harmless lunatic.

CLERVAL: Now you intend to convince them that you're a dangerous lunatic.

FRANKENSTEIN: I only ask them to believe what they see.

CLERVAL: They will hang another label on you. The man who makes monsters.

FRANKENSTEIN: Because the thing is less than beautiful? Heaven knows I used all the skill I had.

CLERVAL: Oh, the face is forgivable. For all I know, a Hottentot may find it handsome. But it has one impossible trait...

FRANKENSTEIN: I'm still listening.

CLERVAL: A new-born mind in a fully developed body.

FRANKENSTEIN: So?

CLERVAL: The result is a wild beast.

FRANKENSTEIN: Prove it.

CLERVAL: How much damage must it do before you're convinced? You said once that a failure could be destroyed...

FRANKENSTEIN: Are you asking me to destroy him?

CLERVAL: For your own safety.

FRANKENSTEIN: But he's alive. Alive!

CLERVAL: So are sharks, adders, tarantula spiders.

FRANKENSTEIN: A living human being.

CLERVAL: An accident. A freak.

FRANKENSTEIN: And I should...

CLERVAL: Kill it.

FRANKENSTEIN: Murder?

CLERVAL: Undo what you have done.

FRANKENSTEIN: I have created life. I will not destroy it.

CLERVAL: You have suspended the laws of nature, Frankenstein. What follows is beyond logic. I can't argue. I can only tell you what I feel. Destroy that thing before it destroys you.

THE CREATURE *shuffles into the cellar.* FRANKENSTEIN, *with his back to the door, does not see it.*

FRANKENSTEIN: Prejudice. Blind prejudice. I'm disappointed in you. Clerval. I'll be more reasonable. I'm prepared to be convinced. Give me one shred of reason why my creation should not exist, and I'll do as you demand—bury my failure under these flagstones.

CLERVAL (*slowly and calmly*): Don't move.

THE CREATURE *puts out its hand, and grasps* FRANKENSTEIN'S *shoulder. It turns him to face it. It strokes* FRANKENSTEIN'S *shoulder affectionately.*

CLERVAL (*bursting out in spite of himself*): Send it away.

FRANKENSTEIN *gently takes* THE CREATURE'S *hand from his shoulder.* THE CREATURE *stands staring at* FRANKENSTEIN, *its arms hanging limply by its side.*

FRANKENSTEIN: Over there.

THE CREATURE *obeys.*

FRANKENSTEIN: You see! He understands.

CLERVAL: You've just given it food and drink. The response looks like gratitude. Now come away.

FRANKENSTEIN: Afraid of putting your theories to the test?

CLERVAL: Confound it all, I am afraid. Not for my theories —for my neck. Call me childish if you like, but if it advances, I shall scream. What is more, it can smell my fear.

FRANKENSTEIN: I can protect you. Look.

He puts his arm around CLERVAL'S *shoulder, and speaks to* THE CREATURE.

FRANKENSTEIN: This—is my friend. Anything that harms him, harms me.

THE CREATURE *snarls, and shambles forward menacingly.* CLERVAL *retreats.*

FRANKENSTEIN: Back.

THE CREATURE *stops, bewildered.*

FRANKENSTEIN: Back.

THE CREATURE *shuffles back.*

CLERVAL: Bravo. I withdraw one charge. The creature feels human emotions. It's jealous. You must be careful how you show affection, Frankenstein. It could prove fatal.

FRANKENSTEIN: That's absurd.

CLERVAL: Is it? . . . Take this poppet.

FRANKENSTEIN: Why?

CLERVAL: I'm not afraid of putting my theories to the test . . . Make believe the toy is precious to you. Then hand it over to your creation. If the thing is gentle towards the doll, it may know what gentleness is.

FRANKENSTEIN: Is this another joke?

CLERVAL: Don't you want to risk a proof?

FRANKENSTEIN: I . . .

CLERVAL: It's watching us. What goes on behind those dead eyes? . . . Here—take the doll.

Awkwardly, quite certain that CLERVAL *is making a fool of him,* FRANKENSTEIN *takes the doll. He shows it to* THE CREATURE, *then cradles it in his arms, and rocks it.* THE CREATURE *growls, and takes a few steps towards* FRANKENSTEIN, *then stops and stares dully.*

FRANKENSTEIN *caresses the doll for a few seconds, then offers it to* THE CREATURE.

THE CREATURE *takes it, and looks at it wonderingly for a few seconds. Then it cradles the doll in a grotesque parody of* FRANKENSTEIN's *action.*

FRANKENSTEIN *turns triumphantly to* CLERVAL. CLERVAL *continues to watch* THE CREATURE. *Slowly and deliberately* THE CREATURE *raises the doll, then with one jerk, pulls the head from the body.*

ACT TWO

Scene Three

CLERVAL'S HOUSE

FRANKENSTEIN *paces the room.* CLERVAL *toying with* FRANKENSTEIN'S *cane, watches him.*

CLERVAL: This house is full of clocks. Great grandfather clocks. Dainty ormulu clocks. Solemn striking clocks. Tinkling little toys. But they all say the same thing.

FRANKENSTEIN: It's late.

CLERVAL: The time will come when it's too late.

FRANKENSTEIN: Why were these rooms made so small? Ten steps and I face a blank wall: turnabout, another ten steps, another blank wall. Blank walls. Torments.

CLERVAL: Your indecision torments you.

FRANKENSTEIN: My doubts frighten me. What am I? Turncoat? Traitor? Judas? If I could be sure.

CLERVAL: I'm involved, too. Do you think it doesn't hurt me to see you hurt?

FRANKENSTEIN: I don't ask for sympathy.

CLERVAL: That creature can bend iron bars. How long will the bolts on the cellar door hold?

FRANKENSTEIN: The laboratory's a ruin. It will take months to rebuild. Then, even if everything comes to hand, a year will have passed before the attempt can be made again. I was ready for the achievement now. This blow . . .

CLERVAL: Is only to your pride.

FRANKENSTEIN: *He* is all I have left.

CLERVAL: If that creature is seen, the attempt will never be made again.

FRANKENSTEIN: Meaning?

CLERVAL: The argument I dare hardly use. Once the ordinary man man realises that you can loose monsters upon him...

FRANKENSTEIN: I do not make monsters.

CLERVAL: Nightwalkers, then.

FRANKENSTEIN: I do not...

CLERVAL: Uglies.

FRANKENSTEIN: Make...

CLERVAL: Anything beyond understanding.

FRANKENSTEIN: Monsters. He is not a monster.

CLERVAL: Common man believes what he sees.

FRANKENSTEIN: I'm working for the common good.

CLERVAL: You won't be believed. Not on that evidence. Your experiments will be driven further underground.

FRANKENSTEIN: I've worked in secret before.

CLERVAL: If you're discovered, it will mean either prison or the mad-house.

FRANKENSTEIN: I'm not afraid of being made into a martyr.

CLERVAL: You wouldn't be a martyr. Just a forgotten number on an official record. I believe in you. I want to help you.

FRANKENSTEIN: Help? I cannot be helped. I am alone.

CLERVAL: We are all lonely that way—anyone who reaches above the clouds. Except in loving, perhaps. You're lucky. You have Elizabeth.

FRANKENSTEIN: I bear my burdens alone.

CLERVAL: Poor Victor. You have so much to learn... Here's father coming... Well?

FRANKENSTEIN (*reluctantly*): It must be done.

CLERVAL: Soon?

FRANKENSTEIN: Today.

CLERVAL: When?

FRANKENSTEIN: Now.

CLERVAL: How?

FRANKENSTEIN: Poison.

CLERVAL: Shall I come with you?

FRANKENSTEIN: No.

CLERVAL: You'll need assistance.

FRANKENSTEIN: I was alone when he first breathed: I'll be alone when . . .

CLERVAL: His grave?

FRANKENSTEIN: A hollow under the flagstones. I made it in case—anything should have to be hidden.

CLERVAL: You may not ask, but you do have my sympathy.

CLERVAL SENIOR *enters with* ELIZABETH.

CLERVAL SNR: There you are.

FRANKENSTEIN (*with a sad attempt at cheerfulness*): Here I am.

CLERVAL SNR.: And almost recovered. Look at the colour in his cheeks again. Elizabeth's nursing. You've a lot to thank Elizabeth for.

ELIZABETH: Frankenstein has no need to thank me.

CLERVAL SNR.: You must take it easy now, my boy. Overwork. Dangerous. It's this climate of ours. Bracing, but over-exciting. Impossible to relax here. You ought to throw everything overboard, and go with young Henri to Italy.

FRANKENSTEIN: Italy?

CLERVAL: Italy.

FRANKENSTEIN: Why—Italy?

CLERVAL: Why does any poet go to Italy? To widen my experience—ancient ruins, and olive-skinned beauties.

FRANKENSTEIN: I didn't know.

CLERVAL: I hardly had the chance to tell you. I could hardly interrupt you in mid-fever, and say "By the way, talking of temperature, I'm on my way to the South."

CLERVAL SNR.: I just can't understand young people these days.

CLERVAL: They're pretty much like the old ones in those days.

CLERVAL SNR.: There's so much that I can't understand . . . Frankenstein, and Elizabeth now. Why look at each other like that? Time enough for that sort of chill when you've been married for fifty years. Confound it, you're not strangers.

JUSTINE *runs in, laughing. She stops, confused, on seeing the group.*

CLERVAL SNR.: Did anyone ring?

JUSTINE: Beg pardon, sir. I could've swore I saw Master William run in here.

CLERVAL SNR.: So you chased after him, eh?

JUSTINE: We were playing, sir. I'm sorry.

CLERVAL SNR.: Playing?

JUSTINE: Shall I go now, sir?

CLERVAL: Don't keep young William hiding too long.

JUSTINE: No, sir.

ELIZABETH: I'll come with you . . . If you'll excuse me.

ELIZABETH *goes out with* JUSTINE.

CLERVAL SENIOR *looks from* FRANKENSTEIN *to the departing* ELIZABETH

CLERVAL SNR.: Well, now!

CLERVAL (*diverting his father's attention*): Poor Justine.

CLERVAL SNR.: Justine?

CLERVAL: She has to apologise now when she plays with her child.

CLERVAL SNR.: She's employed as nurse for him.

CLERVAL: He's growing up. Soon he'll think of her merely as—nurse.

CLERVAL SNR.: Well?

CLERVAL: Poor Justine . . . Still here, Frankenstein?

CLERVAL SNR.: There's politeness for you!

CLERVAL: Frankenstein has been called away on an urgent errand. Will you wait until the clocks strike again? . . . Oh, my flask.

FRANKENSTEIN: Why?

CLERVAL: The fatal dose. It will need disguising.

FRANKENSTEIN: A flask. Deadly innocence. This does frighten me.

CLERVAL SNR.: If neither of you intends to talk anything but nonsense, I'll go to the one room where I can expect to hear sense—the nursery.

He goes out.

CLERVAL: I'll join you, father . . . Frankenstein, I cannot bear pain—even in others. Let it be swift.

FRANKENSTEIN: It will be. It must be done?

CLERVAL: It must be done . . . Not so fast, father.

He hurries after CLERVAL SNR.

FRANKENSTEIN: It must be done.

ACT TWO

Scene Four

THE CELLAR

FRANKENSTEIN *is alone, holding the flask.*

THE CREATURE *shuffles into the cellar.* FRANKENSTEIN *turns to face it.*

After a pause FRANKENSTEIN *makes a gesture of drinking from the flask, then holds it out to* THE CREATURE. *Slowly* THE CREATURE *takes the flask.* FRANKENSTEIN *repeats the gesture of drinking.* THE CREATURE *raises the flask to its mouth. Before it has time to drink, however,* FRANKENSTEIN *knocks the flask from its hand.*

FRANKENSTEIN: No! Leave this place. Hide. Go to the mountains. Go.

THE CREATURE *stares at him uncomprehendingly.*

FRANKENSTEIN: Do I have to kill you? Go. (*Striking at the* CREATURE *with his cane.*) Go. Go. Go. Go.

THE CREATURE *advances upon him furiously, and wrenches the cane from him.*

FRANKENSTEIN *cowers back.*

THE CREATURE *breaks the cane in half, then turns away, and giving animal cries of despair, stumbles out.*

ACT TWO

Scene Five

CLERVAL'S HOUSE

Enter CLERVAL, *dressed for travelling.* FRANKENSTEIN *walks moodily with him.*

CLERVAL: Brr. No fires in these rooms. Is the house in mourning because I'm leaving? . . . Here's a list of my addresses. As long as I avoid coach wrecks and avalanches, we should keep in touch . . . The coach leaves in half an hour.

FRANKENSTEIN: This is goodbye, then.

CLERVAL: Au revoir. You did promise to write.

FRANKENSTEIN: Regularly.

CLERVAL (*looking through the window*): Winter is here with a vengeance. A stray animal forced its way into the grounds last night. Father was out before breakfast this morning, examining the snow. He thinks it may have been a wolf.

FRANKENSTEIN: A wolf?

CLERVAL: The bitter weather brings them close to the town. And here I am on my way to the South.

FRANKENSTEIN: Of course. A wolf.

CLERVAL: But there was snow brushed away from the branches of the tree outside my window. Have you ever seen a wolf climb trees?

FRANKENSTEIN: What was it then?

CLERVAL: Don't look so pale. Not a ghost. Only a cat . . . Look after yourself. You do look haunted.

FRANKENSTEIN: I am haunted. I hear things. I—see—things. The footprint. The handprint. The shadow.

CLERVAL: The experiment *is* ended. Isn't it?

FRANKENSTEIN: All over.

CLERVAL: Dead and buried?

FRANKENSTEIN: I buried—my journal—in the cellar.

CLERVAL: Capital. We'll be proud of you yet . . . They're calling for me. (*Goes to door.*)

FRANKENSTEIN: Clerval . . .

CLERVAL: Yes?

FRANKENSTEIN: It might have been . . .

CLERVAL: What?

FRANKENSTEIN: A—a wolf.

CLERVAL: It might. But it wasn't.

FRANKENSTEIN: What was it then?

CLERVAL: I told you—a cat . . . I'll see you in the summer.

CLERVAL goes out.

FRANKENSTEIN: It *is* ended. I buried my books.

But he swings round, as though he hears a sound behind him, almost expecting some horror to emerge from a dark corner.

FRANKENSTEIN (*firmly, to convince himself*): It *is* ended.

He follows CLERVAL.

ACT TWO

Scene Six

CLERVAL'S HOUSE

Music in the next room. MME. COUPER *enters with* ELIZABETH.

MME. COUPER: Not here either? Where does the man hide? You really must keep a closer watch, my dear. One of these days he'll be slipping away for ever.

ELIZABETH: Frankenstein is free to do as he pleases.

MME. COUPER: Noble sentiments, my dear, but dangerous. Men are like sheep—always straying if given half a chance. Other meadows are so attractive.

ELIZABETH: I should imagine the easiest way to lose any man would be to tie him by apron strings.

MME. COUPER: Maybe so. But if I were you, I'd keep a close watch on him. You don't want to be deserted before you're a bride. You *are* to be a bride very soon?

ELIZABETH: No.

MME. COUPER: No?

ELIZABETH: The wedding has been—postponed.

MME. COUPER: You don't mean that Frankenstein has deserted you already?

ELIZABETH: Postponed until Clerval returns from Italy.

MME. COUPER: Well, everything comes to him who waits. They say . . . I do believe the music has ended. I adore these musical evenings at the Clerval house. They are the only reason for staying in this dreary town during January. If the music has finished, we really must return.

ELIZABETH (*at the window*): Oh!

MME. COUPER: What is the matter?

ELIZABETH: Down there. I saw a shadow moving about the garden.

MME. COUPER: A wolf!

ELIZABETH: Upright?

MME. COUPER: A man, then.

ELIZABETH: Perhaps. Very tall, though.

MME. COUPER: Probably Frankenstein.

ELIZABETH: Of course. Frankenstein.

ACT TWO

FRANKENSTEIN *enters. He watches the two ladies without speaking.*

ELIZABETH: Or a cloud across the moon.

MME. COUPER (*joining her at the window*): High up here, from this window one can see clear to the road. Nothing . . . If you don't join Frankenstein this instant, I'll declare you don't deserve him.

FRANKENSTEIN: He is here.

MME. COUPER: Well! . . . Well, well, well . . . There you are . . . Now I really am de trop. Don't put yourselves out on my account. Please. I shall go down to supper. They always serve supper after the music. So delighted to see you re-united.

As she makes for the door, music starts again. She stops undecided.

FRANKENSTEIN: An encore. Supper will be served immediately afterwards.

MME. COUPER: So hospitable!

She goes out. ELIZABETH *holds out her hands to* FRANKENSTEIN. *He crosses to her.*

FRANKENSTEIN: Elizabeth.

ELIZABETH: Victor?

After a slight hesitation, he kisses her.

FRANKENSTEIN: I love you, Elizabeth. I do love you.

ELIZABETH: I want so much to believe you.

FRANKENSTEIN: Then what is there to prevent our plans from becoming facts?

ELIZABETH: In the Spring? Clerval . . .

FRANKENSTEIN: In the spring. In the summer. This time next year. The date's not important. What does matter is the excuse you'll find for postponing it again—and again —and again.

ELIZABETH: You don't understand, do you? If you came near to understanding, it might be possible. I love you, too, my dear, but . . .

FRANKENSTEIN: What is that but?

ELIZABETH: When we were young, we seemed to laugh with one voice, think with one mind. Then it was inevitable that we should marry. Now . . .

FRANKENSTEIN: We are the same people.

ELIZABETH: Are we?

FRANKENSTEIN: This is my face. Touch it. See.

ELIZABETH: I can't touch you. You're wrapped in armour.

FRANKENSTEIN: A silly romantic whim. You've read too many of Clerval's verses.

ELIZABETH: It's called pride, Frankenstein.

FRANKENSTEIN: Pride?

ELIZABETH: It cuts you off from the world. From me.

FRANKENSTEIN: I've gone down among the filth of the slums to relieve the wretched—is that pride? I've lived among death and corruption—is that pride? I defied the cries of scandal when I took in Justine and her child—was that pride?

ELIZABETH: Pride.

FRANKENSTEIN: The word has a different meaning for each of us.

ELIZABETH: You see—you don't understand me.

FRANKENSTEIN: There is nothing but illusion parting us. What must I do to persuade you?

ELIZABETH: Repeat every day after your prayers "It is sometimes more blessed to receive than to give". When you believe that, our marriage may be possible.

FRANKENSTEIN: Very well: I believe you. Prove me. What

must I request? It's one of the penalties of a more than adequate income that I've so little to ask for.

ELIZABETH: You need not even ask. Just accept.

FRANKENSTEIN: What?

ELIZABETH: Help.

FRANKENSTEIN: How?

ELIZABETH: I know what you were doing as I waited here.

FRANKENSTEIN: Yes?

ELIZABETH: You were searching the house from attic to cellar, examining every room, checking every latch and bolt.

FRANKENSTEIN: Well?

ELIZABETH: Why?

FRANKENSTEIN: An—itch. An urge. A sudden fancy. I'm sleeping here tonight.

ELIZABETH: Yesterday, as we walked by the river, you kept glancing over your shoulder. Were we followed? When a shadow fell across the path, you started as though it were a snake . . . No answer?

FRANKENSTEIN: You mustn't ask. You must never ask.

ELIZABETH: You see?

FRANKENSTEIN: There is nothing wrong. Absolutely nothing.

ELIZABETH: Are you sure?

FRANKENSTEIN: Nothing, I said. I meant nothing.

ELIZABETH: What use is a wife unless she can share your burdens?

FRANKENSTEIN: I cannot pass my troubles on to you.

ELIZABETH: Then you are troubled.

FRANKENSTEIN: No.

ELIZABETH: Do you understand me now? There could never be a marriage on those terms. It may sound silly and trivial, but it is neither silly nor trivial to me. Even after the ceremony we should be mere acquaintances—not husband and wife.

Pause.

FRANKENSTEIN: If it must be, then it must be. What I know, I must know alone. Whatever threatens must threaten me alone. It may be that I must live and die alone.

ELIZABETH: Victor, I want . . . Can't you see that I want . . .

FRANKENSTEIN *takes her in his arms, and kisses her.*

There is a scream, off.

FRANKENSTEIN: Good God!

He hurries to the door.

ELIZABETH: Take me with you.

FRANKENSTEIN: No. Stay here. You'll be safe here. Don't move. Whatever you do, don't move. Just pray that it isn't what I fear. I'll return as soon as I can.

ELIZABETH *waits. The room seems to grow colder.*

There is a hysterical whimpering, off. ELIZABETH *turns to face the door.* MME. COUPER *comes in.*

MME. COUPER: Elizabeth! Oh, Elizabeth, my dear.

ELIZABETH: What is it?

MME. COUPER: Justine. Justine.

ELIZABETH: What has happened to Justine?

MME. COUPER: She has—murdered—the child.

ELIZABETH: You're hysterical.

MME. COUPER: She was found with him. Blood. Blood everywhere. And the poor boy dead on his bed.

ELIZABETH: That can't be true.

MME. COUPER: The thought! I shan't sleep tonight. I'll never sleep again. If one can't trust the servants . . .

ELIZABETH: It mustn't be true.

MME. COUPER: Smelling salts. Brandy.

She collapses into a chair, and has an attack of whimpering hysteria.

ELIZABETH: Control yourself—please.

MME. COUPER: He was her child. She couldn't bear to see the proof of her sin. She killed him.

ELIZABETH: May Heaven forgive you for . . .

CLERVAL SNR. *enters.*

ELIZABETH: M. Clerval, can you hear what is being said?

CLERVAL SNR.: I heard.

ELIZABETH: Then say it's a lie.

CLERVAL SNR.: I wish I could. William is dead. Justine is accused.

ELIZABETH: Justine? No.

She runs from the room.

CLERVAL SNR.: A lifetime spent judging men has taught me that I know very little about the human heart. I put all my trust in evidence now. But it is black against her.

MME. COUPER: That girl must be brought to justice. The sight! My stomach turned right over.

CLERVAL SNR.: Come with me. You'll be more at ease with the rest of the company.

MME. COUPER: Feel how I am trembling. My arm . . .

CLERVAL SNR.: I've a medicine downstairs to cure that. Take my arm.

He takes MME. COUPER's *arm. As they go out they pass* FRANKENSTEIN *and* JUSTINE *in the doorway.*

FRANKENSTEIN: There. Please, Justine. Please.

JUSTINE *controls herself with an effort, but stares straight ahead, not seeing anyone.*

FRANKENSTEIN: Now you must let me help you . . . What happened?

JUSTINE: I—I . . .

FRANKENSTEIN: Yes, I know it hurts you to think of it. I'm sorry. But you must tell me.

JUSTINE: I can't.

FRANKENSTEIN: Think. Think. Unless I know, I'm helpless.

JUSTINE: I can't remember.

FRANKENSTEIN: You must try. Before the police arrive.

JUSTINE: The police?

FRANKENSTEIN: There's little I can do once they take you away.

JUSTINE: They'll take me away? Prison? I—didn't . . . Believe me. Please believe me.

FRANKENSTEIN: I do. But I must prove it. What happened?

JUSTINE: I don't know. I don't know.

FRANKENSTEIN: You put William to bed. When? The time?

JUSTINE: After you kissed him goodnight.

FRANKENSTEIN: The details. You must remember every trifle. The details may be forgotten in an hour, and they're important.

JUSTINE: He—said his prayers, like I taught him. He stumbled once, as though he'd forgotten, but he hadn't.

FRANKENSTEIN: Yes. Yes. Every detail.

JUSTINE: I can't.

FRANKENSTEIN: I must discover what happened. What really happened. He said his prayers.

JUSTINE: Then he climbed into bed. The church bells down in the town began to ring, and he asked me to open the window so that he could hear them.

FRANKENSTEIN: You opened the window. What did you see?

JUSTINE: The snow, smooth as a sheet. Then I kissed him goodnight, and left the room. I left the door open.

FRANKENSTEIN: Why?

JUSTINE: You're staying the night, sir. He hoped you'd look in before you went to bed yourself. Your room is next to his.

FRANKENSTEIN: The room next to mine. An open window. An open invitation.

JUSTINE: I heard a noise. A scuffling and half a sob. I didn't know what it might be, so I went back.

FRANKENSTEIN: What did you find?

JUSTINE: I couldn't see anything. It was as though a black thing by the window shut out all the light. Then it was gone—through the window or into thin air, I don't know. I wouldn't expect anybody to believe that.

FRANKENSTEIN: I do.

JUSTINE: As soon as the moon come streaming into the room again, I saw the bed. The boy looked asleep, but after I touched him my hands were . . . I don't know how long I stood. They found me like that.

   CLERVAL SNR. *enters with* ELIZABETH.

FRANKENSTEIN: I understand now.

JUSTINE: What will become of me?

CLERVAL SNR.: Justine.

JUSTINE: You've come to take me away?

CLERVAL SNR.: There are—some gentlemen here. They want to—to talk with you.

JUSTINE: Will they believe me?

CLERVAL SNR.: If you've done no wrong.

JUSTINE: If they don't believe me? What will they do then?

There is no reply. JUSTINE *crosses in silence to* CLERVAL SNR.

FRANKENSTEIN: You'll come to no harm.

JUSTINE: Is it cold in that place? Will they let me take my shawl?

FRANKENSTEIN: Set your mind at ease. You'll be safe, Justine. I give my solemn word.

JUSTINE: I trust you, sir . . . I'm ready now.

CLERVAL SNR.: Only tell the truth, my dear, and you've nothing to worry about.

He takes JUSTINE *out with him.*

ELIZABETH: William dead, and Justine arrested. No. Not in this house. Not with the church bells ringing, and the music tinkling. If it were true, could I stand here so calmly?

FRANKENSTEIN: Do you believe Justine?

ELIZABETH: I know her.

FRANKENSTEIN: If she were a stranger, would you believe her?

ELIZABETH: No.

FRANKENSTEIN: Then I must save her myself.

ELIZABETH (*warning*): Victor.

FRANKENSTEIN: Even though I ruin myself doing it.

ELIZABETH: Think of what you are saying.

FRANKENSTEIN: She's worth the sacrifice.

ELIZABETH: Not that. That is not what I mean.

FRANKENSTEIN: Pen and paper.

ELIZABETH: For a few seconds you were the man I once knew.

FRANKENSTEIN: I must write to Clerval.

ELIZABETH: Now the fires are burning in your eyes again.

FRANKENSTEIN: He must return. Immediately. He is the only other person in the world who knows the murderer.

ELIZABETH: Listen, Victor. Please listen to me.

FRANKENSTEIN: With Clerval's evidence to support me I can stay the trial before it begins.

ELIZABETH: William is dead.

FRANKENSTEIN: I'll make sure that justice is done.

ELIZABETH: The prison is a foul place: Justine will be locked there tonight. One has suffered: the other is suffering. Does their pain mean nothing more than your triumph?

FRANKENSTEIN: Triumph?

ELIZABETH: You'll avenge William and deliver Justine. Oh, yes, I believe you when you say you can. And you'll be —so—proud. But I would almost have you fail, and know that there was pity and understanding in your heart.

FRANKENSTEIN: Your face is so hard.

ELIZABETH: Our faces reflect our thoughts, don't they?

FRANKENSTEIN: You can't guess what this gesture will cost me.

ELIZABETH: Look at yourself. Go to the mirror and look at yourself. Unless you're afraid to see Lucifer.

FRANKENSTEIN: Elizabeth!

ELIZABETH: I'm sorry. Disappointment made me want to hurt you.

FRANKENSTEIN: What do you want from me?

ELIZABETH: *From* you? Nothing.

FRANKENSTEIN: Am I so vicious?

ELIZABETH: Oh, my dear, who can say when virtue becomes a vice? Write your letters. The glory will be all yours.

FRANKENSTEIN: I can't turn back.

ELIZABETH: No. You must go on.

She turns abruptly, and leaves the room.

FRANKENSTEIN *dips his pen into the ink, and begins to write.*

FRANKENSTEIN: My dear Clerval . . .

ACT TWO

Scene Seven

CLERVAL'S HOUSE

FRANKENSTEIN *is waiting impatiently.* CLERVAL SNR. *enters.*

CLERVAL SNR.: Hope I've not kept you waiting, my boy.

FRANKENSTEIN: I've been waiting for weeks: another hour makes little difference.

CLERVAL SNR.: I was at the court-room all day. I suddenly realise that I'm an old man. Once I was interested in the parade of human vanity: now I'm dismayed by it.

FRANKENSTEIN: The news, sir. What news?

CLERVAL SNR.: The process of the law grinds on. Her trial begins tomorrow.

FRANKENSTEIN: But Clerval. Surely you've heard of him by now.

CLERVAL SNR.: Haven't you?

FRANKENSTEIN: Not a word. I can't understand it.

CLERVAL SNR.: Then I'm more fortunate. I had a package this morning.

FRANKENSTEIN: What does it say?

CLERVAL SNR.: Nothing.

FRANKENSTEIN: Nothing?

CLERVAL SNR.: The scenery inspiring, the weather improving, the natives rogues, his companions bearable.

FRANKENSTEIN: When does he return?

CLERVAL SNR.: Try to compose yourself. Accidents happen.

FRANKENSTEIN: I told him that Justine's life depended on it.

CLERVAL SNR.: He met an English poet. They travelled to Florence and Genoa instead of Verona and Venice. Everything we addressed to him miscarried.

FRANKENSTEIN: But Justine ...

CLERVAL SNR.: The trial begins tomorrow.

FRANKENSTEIN: It must be stopped.

CLERVAL SNR.: My dear young man ...

FRANKENSTEIN: Delayed.

CLERVAL SNR.: The Office of Justice is a heavy piece of machinery. Once it is set in motion ...

FRANKENSTEIN: Justine must not stand trial tomorrow. It's unthinkable.

CLERVAL SNR.: She will.

FRANKENSTEIN: But the verdict is a foregone conclusion. Without my evidence, supported by Clerval, any jury must find her guilty.

CLERVAL SNR.: I hate to admit it, but I see no other answer.

FRANKENSTEIN: She is not guilty.

CLERVAL SNR.: She was the only person in the room with the child. The snow beneath the window was unmarked.

FRANKENSTEIN: I know that. But I know more than you. Even without Clerval I must go to the Public Prosecutor. This murderer didn't walk on the ground.

CLERVAL SNR.: An interesting theory.

FRANKENSTEIN: He has the appearance of a man, but he is greater than a man. He can bend iron as though it were clay. I thought his only deficiency was intelligence. I was wrong. He haunts me. I no longer see him—just a dead bird in my path, a sprig of eidelweiss on my window-sill, the print of a hand on the wall—but he haunts me. I once did him a great wrong. God forgive us both, I can't blame him. But the intended victim that night was not William. It was myself.

CLERVAL SNR.: Go on.

FRANKENSTEIN: There is no more to say.

CLERVAL SNR.: The Public Prosecutor will have more to say if you bring this forward as evidence. Where can this creature be found?

FRANKENSTEIN: In the mountains.

CLERVAL SNR.: Whereabouts?

FRANKENSTEIN: I don't know. In some cave or hollow.

CLERVAL SNR.: How do you know this?

FRANKENSTEIN: Because I . . . I—was—responsible for him.

CLERVAL SNR.: Ah. Then who else might bring evidence?

FRANKENSTEIN: Clerval.

CLERVAL SNR.: Besides Clerval. The man must have friends, acquaintances.

FRANKENSTEIN: No one.

CLERVAL SNR.: Even someone else who has seen him then.

FRANKENSTEIN: No one.

CLERVAL SNR.: That answer's impossibly negative. The man doesn't exist who has only been seen by two people.

FRANKENSTEIN: This—creature has been seen only by Clerval and myself.

CLERVAL SNR.: Clerval is in another country.

FRANKENSTEIN: I know. I know.

CLERVAL SNR.: And this is the story you intend to present to a jury? An unknown monster that swoops in the night without leaving a trace.

Pause.

CLERVAL SNR.: You'd go to any lengths to save Justine.

FRANKENSTEIN: I mean to.

CLERVAL SNR.: Don't.

FRANKENSTEIN: I must.

CLERVAL SNR.: You'll be laughed out of court.

FRANKENSTEIN: You don't believe me. Even you are convinced that Justine . . .

CLERVAL SNR.: Thank God I'm not required to judge this case.

FRANKENSTEIN: Suppose—the trial goes against her. How long?

CLERVAL SNR.: A few weeks, perhaps.

FRANKENSTEIN: But a journey to Italy takes all of that time.

CLERVAL SNR.: We must all live with our consciences, and trust that justice is done. Now give yourself a respite. You'll join us for dinner?

FRANKENSTEIN: The trial must be postponed. Without Clerval it will be a mockery.

CLERVAL SNR.: It will start tomorrow.

ACT TWO

Scene Eight

THE CELLAR

FRANKENSTEIN *stumbles in, throws himself upon the ground, and lies there, sobbing.*

A dark shadow materialises just outside the circle of light from his lamp. Eventually FRANKENSTEIN *becomes aware of it. He scrambles to his feet.*

The shadow moves forward. FRANKENSTEIN *backs.*

SHADOW: The scene of the crime?

FRANKENSTEIN: Clerval!

CLERVAL: A last minute rescue?

FRANKENSTEIN: But how——? When . . . ?

CLERVAL: I posted from Genoa the same hour that I heard. I left half my baggage at the pensione.

FRANKENSTEIN: There was no letter.

CLERVAL: My mail-coach travelled as fast as anything I could have written. I even ran to the courthouse. You created a sensation.

FRANKENSTEIN: You heard the sentence?

CLERVAL: Yes.

FRANKENSTEIN: Fourteen days to live. That is called Justice. Justice! Heaven keep me from justice like that.

CLERVAL: You may prefer that justice to Heaven's. Your letter was so terse I had to fill in most of the details myself. Is Justine innocent?

FRANKENSTEIN: You know she is.

CLERVAL: The alternative is just as disagreeable. It means that you are a murderer.

FRANKENSTEIN: No.

CLERVAL: Where did you bury the body? Under which flagstone?

FRANKENSTEIN: I—couldn't. I—turned it loose.

CLERVAL: I warned you. Fool. You realise what must be done now. Either Justine must be hanged, or you and I must tell the whole story.

FRANKENSTEIN: I tried. The result was laughter and sneers. Why else do you think I sent for you?

CLERVAL: Couldn't you have caught the creature? What more evidence would you have needed?

FRANKENSTEIN: One man—hunt it alone? You're mistaken

in the balance of power. The strong hunts the weak. I'm not the hunter: I'm the victim.

CLERVAL: Of that animal?

FRANKENSTEIN: Its cunning grows day by day. I can feel its presence like an evil spell. It will never leave as long as I am alive.

CLERVAL: You're not its intended victim.

FRANKENSTEIN: It hates me. One day it will have its revenge.

CLERVAL: I said nothing about revenge. But it won't touch you. It worshipped you. Your nearest and dearest are the ones in danger.

FRANKENSTEIN: William's death was a mistake.

CLERVAL: William was only the first victim. The monster intends to leave you desolate—as you left it.

FRANKENSTEIN: How do you know?

CLERVAL: I put myself in its place. It's what I'd do if I were—a monster. As soon as Justine is safe, the creature must be killed. And this time I'll make sure there is no backsliding. After all, I don't want to be sacrificed for our friendship. I've too much to live for.

FRANKENSTEIN: As you say.

CLERVAL: And I've another condition. It may destroy our friendship, but I insist.

FRANKENSTEIN: Well?

CLERVAL: You must abandon your researches entirely.

FRANKENSTEIN: Oh, no!

CLERVAL: No more half-men.

FRANKENSTEIN: Give me a year . . . The next experiment—or the next . . .

CLERVAL: There will never be another experiment.

FRANKENSTEIN: I buried my books. Isn't that enough?

CLERVAL: Burn them.

FRANKENSTEIN: Later.

CLERVAL: Now.

FRANKENSTEIN: While we are arguing, Justine needs us.

CLERVAL: I shall go to Justine as soon as I have your promise.

FRANKENSTEIN: How can you be so hard?

CLERVAL: I surprise myself.

FRANKENSTEIN (*reluctantly*): Very well.

CLERVAL: Swear?

FRANKENSTEIN: I swear.

CLERVAL: Where are the books?

FRANKENSTEIN: Under this flagstone.

CLERVAL: I had your promise once before. If I left you to temptation, I'd be guilty of your perjury. Leave me to destroy them.

FRANKENSTEIN: No.

CLERVAL: You intend to be forsworn already? Go to Justine. She needs you. Tell her the worst ordeal is over.

FRANKENSTEIN: Don't be long.

FRANKENSTEIN *leaves.* CLERVAL *goes to the doorway to see him on his way, then turns back into the cellar. He takes off his hat, wipes his brow, and replaces his hat again. Then he walks over to where* FRANKENSTEIN *was standing, and kneels down. He feels around the edge of a flagstone. It is obviously loose. He is about to pull at it when he hears a noise. He straightens and listens.*

CLERVAL: Frankenstein?

He stands up. He hears the noise repeated, and goes towards it.

CLERVAL: Who's there?

He goes out. There is a muffled cry. Pause. THE CREATURE *enters, carrying* CLERVAL'S *hat* ...

ACT TWO

Scene Nine

PRISON

JUSTINE *is sitting on a stool, alone. A door is opened with a clatter of bolts and chains.*

ELIZABETH *enters.*

ELIZABETH: Justine!

JUSTINE *gets up joyfully, then remembers where she is. She sits again, and hangs her head.*

ELIZABETH: Why do you turn from me?

JUSTINE: How can I look at anybody again?

ELIZABETH: You've done nothing.

JUSTINE: The faces in the court-room—all eyes—all staring.

ELIZABETH: Sensual creatures, smacking their lips at the prospect of another victim. The shame is theirs.

JUSTINE: I don't blame them. Everything seemed so natural—the way it was brought out, bit by bit, until I was almost believing it myself. Then the disgrace crept into me.

ELIZABETH: Justine. Look at me.

JUSTINE: Why?

ELIZABETH: Because we are friends.

JUSTINE: You oughtn't to be here, miss. This is the place they keep for—for them who aren't fit to live.

ELIZABETH: Because I have to keep despair away.

JUSTINE: You don't have to worry, miss. The gaoler talked to me. He promised I wouldn't be hurt much. He said it would all be over before I knew anything about it.

ELIZABETH: Surely not!

JUSTINE: Oh, he meant it kindly. If he seemed a bit rough, it's because he's a rough man. You see, he spends all his life here. He didn't want me to be frightened. These walls are covered with names—scratched there by men and women who were here before me. All waiting.

ELIZABETH: Don't think of them.

JUSTINE: I'm one of them.

ELIZABETH: No. No. No.

JUSTINE: I'm ready to go. My conscience is clear.

ELIZABETH: You mustn't think like this.

JUSTINE: I was always taught not to be afraid of dying.

ELIZABETH: It's wicked. It's wasteful.

JUSTINE: What is there for me to live for? He was all I had in the world. He's gone. What else is there to keep me? I'm only sorry that folk should think wrong of me. But, as the gaoler says, come next year, nobody's like to remember.

ELIZABETH: Oh, Justine . . .

JUSTINE: Tears, miss? That's wrong.

ELIZABETH: I have only five minutes to bring something like comfort, and . . .

JUSTINE: It's you that needs comforting, miss. Don't you believe in Heaven?

The door clanks open again.

FRANKENSTEN (*calling back as he enters*): Confound your regulations. I'll take the responsibility. Justine . . .

JUSTINE (*standing*): Sir?

FRANKENSTEIN: News. Good news . . . It's worth a smile.

JUSTINE: I—don't have the chance to smile much now.

ELIZABETH: Victor. Be careful what you say.

FRANKENSTEIN: Clerval is here. At last we can prove . . . Do you hear?

JUSTINE: I heard, sir.

FRANKENSTEIN: We have enough evidence to demand a new trial.

JUSTINE: No. No.

FRANKENSTEIN: Why not?

JUSTINE: Questions. Questions. Like ropes—twisting and tying 'till you're helpless.

FRANKENSTEIN: This time your defence will be unbreakable.

JUSTINE: My heart isn't, sir.

FRANKENSTEIN: With Clerval's testimony the hearing needn't last an hour. You'll be freed.

JUSTINE: Freed?

FRANKENSTEIN: You won't be kept in this hell-hole a minute longer than I can help. I should have been here sooner, but I had to batter my way past the bureaucratic mind first. I've been delayed for hours in back offices. The wonder is that Clerval wasn't here first. Justine, it means a reprieve. I've done as I promised.

JUSTINE: You must feel very proud, sir.

FRANKENSTEIN: Proud? But—but I've brought new hope.

JUSTINE: I don't want to hope.

FRANKENSTEIN: You can't live without it.

JUSTINE: Hope hurts. Every hope that dies hurts like a little death. I hoped the boy might live; I hoped the men would believe the truth; I hoped the judges would be gentle: I hoped . . . Every hope has been broken. I know what is to happen to me, sir. I'm prepared now. A long sleep, with no more waking and crying in the night.

FRANKENSTEIN: Don't you want to believe me?

JUSTINE: I don't mind prison now. Four walls are four walls anywhere. The shame is all that's left for me to bear, and that's not for long.

FRANKENSTEIN: The whole world will know that you were falsely accused.

JUSTINE: Can I still hope for that?

FRANKENSTEIN: You'll have that, and more.

CLERVAL SNR. enters silently.

FRANKENSTEIN: You've grown thin and pale. We'll take you to the South where the sun can paint roses in your cheeks once more. You'll have time to forget this cruel winter. You'll live again. Clerval will stand up before the judges, and then . . .

CLERVAL SNR.: Clerval will not.

They turn and stare at him.

FRANKENSTEIN: Will—not?

CLERVAL SNR.: Clerval is dead.

FRANKENSTEIN: Clerval!

Quietly, unnoticed, JUSTINE sits.

CLERVAL SNR. (*restoring to officialese to bury his feelings*):

The body was identified by several persons. I, myself, left the mortuary a few minutes ago. The doctor advised us that the back was broken. Death must have been instantaneous.

ELIZABETH (*going to him*): Papa Clerval.

CLERVAL SNR.: My dear.

FRANKENSTEIN: But he was alive when I left him.

CLERVAL SNR.: The officer of the watch discovered the body lying by the roadside in the old quarter of the town. It is assumed that he fell from the high window of a deserted house. The how and why will never be known. But it was an accident.

ELIZABETH: Justine . . .

JUSTINE: I was right, miss. That's all. There's only a little while for me to wait.

FRANKENSTEIN: William. Clerval. Justine. No, not Justine. If nothing less than the body of the murderer can prove her innocence, I'll hunt the creature. I'll neither rest nor sleep until I can throw its carcase at the feet of the judges. My life against his.

He plunges out.

ACT TWO

Scene Ten

CLERVAL'S HOUSE

ELIZABETH *is sitting by the table.* FRANKENSTEIN *enters carrying a box. He looks at her in surprise.*

FRANKENSTEIN: Turn down the light!

ELIZABETH: Victor! Why—?

FRANKENSTEIN (*putting his box on the table*): Turn down the light.

ELIZABETH: You're cold and wet. Hasn't the rain stopped?

FRANKENSTEIN: The light can be seen from the road. (*He turns it down*). Why aren't you in town with Papa Clerval?

ELIZABETH: This is my home.

FRANKENSTEIN: Doesn't he need you? Is he better?

ELIZABETH: Tonight he needs to be alone. Tonight we all need to be alone. That is why I sit here, counting the drops on the windowpane.

FRANKENSTEIN: The rain stopped some time ago. The high wind whips the clouds along. The moon is full.

ELIZABETH: Justine is alone, too. I went to the prison, but I wasn't allowed to see her. I believe the governor was afraid of an attempt to contrive an escape. At least your protests had some effect—they frightened the authorities. Now Justine is guarded like a dangerous animal.

FRANKENSTEIN: Until the morning.

ELIZABETH: Must she die? (*She touches the box*). What is this?

FRANKENSTEIN: Pistols.

ELIZABETH: In the town everyone is convinced that you are mad—hunting a phantom.

FRANKENSTEIN: I've scoured the mountains: there can't be a gully, peak, or crevasse that I haven't covered. But no sign. It *was* there. It does exist. Do you believe me?

ELIZABETH: I believe that Justine is innocent, and that you'd invade the underworld to help her.

FRANKENSTEIN: Do you believe in the creature?

ELIZABETH: I have never seen it.

FRANKENSTEIN: I wish I never had. I created it.

ELIZABETH: Victor, please . . .

FRANKENSTEIN: With my own hands I made it. I brought it to life. And I am not mad. You have seen it.

ELIZABETH: I?

FRANKENSTEIN: That night in the laboratory. The covered thing. You stretched out your hand to touch it. I knocked your arm away. We quarrelled.

ELIZABETH: You brought this thing into the world?

FRANKENSTEIN: Misery and destruction with it. The blame is all mine.

Pause.

ELIZABETH: I must forgive you.

FRANKENSTEIN: Forgive?

ELIZABETH: You weren't to foresee.

FRANKENSTEIN: I didn't ask for forgiveness.

ELIZABETH: You may yet.

FRANKENSTEIN: The responsibility is mine. Mine alone. Your forgiveness would involve you. Would you condone these crimes? No. The crime and the criminal hang together. I won't have anyone share my sins. I'm strong enough to bear them alone. I will be strong . . . Did you hear that? The tapping at the window?

ELIZABETH: A dead twig.

FRANKENSTEIN: You must be brave tonight, Elizabeth. If I had known you'd be here, I'd never have taken the risk. But now . . . the trap is set.

ELIZABETH: What risk?

FRANKENSTEIN: Tonight we shall have a caller—you and I and the echoing house.

ELIZABETH: That—thing?

FRANKENSTEIN: I set a trap—a spring lock, a length of thread, a bell. Absurd to think of a tinkling thing set to catch—That. When the thread breaks, the bell will ring, and the spring lock will have made him a prisoner. We shall meet face to face. I shall try to kill it—the pistols are primed and loaded. But even if I fail, my body will prove what I set out to prove. If the worst happens, as soon as day breaks, you must go to the justices—to Papa Clerval. Tell him everything that you know. It may save Justine . . . Hark!

ELIZABETH: Soot in the chimney. The rain brings it down.

FRANKENSTEIN: Here comes the moon. I promised the moon, didn't I?

ELIZABETH: If the creature is so cunning, is it likely to walk into your trap?

FRANKENSTEIN: The bait is enticing enough. There have been two attempts on my life already. They miscarried because the creature claimed the wrong victim. William and Clerval died instead of me. Could it resist me now—alone and helpless?

ELIZABETH: Up here, above the treetops, alone with the moon, we are outside likelihood.

Pause. FRANKENSTEIN *paces the room.*

FRANKENSTEIN: Wait. Wait.

ELIZABETH: Patience.

FRANKENSTEIN: How many hours are there in a minute?

ELIZABETH: Justine is waiting, too. Does time stand still for her? Suppose the creature doesn't come?

FRANKENSTEIN: He is near now. I can feel the prickling of evil.

ELIZABETH: Poor creature.

FRANKENSTEIN: You feel compassion for it?

ELIZABETH: Spurned by its creator. Solitary among the rocks, wild as the weather. Suppose you were convinced that God had cast you out. No wonder it kills.

FRANKENSTEIN: A board creaked.

ELIZABETH: Still you wait?

FRANKENSTEIN: The trap must work first. There is no room for failure. As soon as I leave this room, you must lock the door behind me. Don't open it until you hear my voice. Make as little sound as you can. You'll be safe in here. (*He takes a pistol from the box.*) Don't worry about me. I'm as prepared as a man can be. It's a pity these things only hold one bullet each.

ELIZABETH: (*impulsively*): Victor—don't!

FRANKENSTEIN: And leave Justine to die? You're right, my dear. I am a proud man. But I know that all my debts must be paid.

In the distance a bell tinkles. FRANKENSTEIN *goes to the door.*

FRANKENSTEIN: Lock the door behind me.

He goes out. ELIZABETH *closes the door behind him, and locks it. She returns immediately with the key. She puts the key on the table. She paces the room for a second or two, then pauses in the corner of the room opposite the window. She bows her head.*

THE CREATURE *comes in through the window. It stands by the table, peering uncertainly about the room.*

Slowly ELIZABETH *realises that she is not alone. She sees* THE CREATURE, *and crosses swiftly to the door.*

The movement attracts the attention of THE CREATURE. *It turns to face her. She realises that the door is locked, and that the key is on the table.*

THE CREATURE *advances slowly.* ELIZABETH *backs towards the table. She feels behind her, and her fingers close on the remaining pistol.*

ELIZABETH: Don't come closer. Don't come closer.

She aims the pistol. THE CREATURE *puts out its arms. She fires.* THE CREATURE *staggers back with a roar of pain and rage, clutching at its chest.* ELIZABETH *escapes to the far corner of the room.* THE CREATURE, *coughing, recovers itself, and begins to advance again.* ELIZABETH *screams.*

FRANKENSTEIN (*off*): Elizabeth! Open the door. Elizabeth!

A shot, off. THE CREATURE *pauses.* FRANKENSTEIN *runs into the room. He raises his pistol, but realises that it is useless now. It drops from his fingers.*

FRANKENSTEIN: Here I am. You hunted me. Here I am.

THE CREATURE *turns again to* ELIZABETH.

FRANKENSTEIN: No!

THE CREATURE *almost reaches* ELIZABETH *when it crashes to the ground.* FRANKENSTEIN *runs to the body, kneels by it, and turns it over.*

FRANKENSTEIN: It—it would have . . .

ELIZABETH: I killed him.

FRANKENSTEIN *looks up at her.*

FRANKENSTEIN: Forgive me. I was—wrong. Forgive me.

ELIZABETH *draws him towards her, comforting him.*

ELIZABETH: Victor, my dear. (*She glances at* THE CREATURE.) Poor thing. It had to die so that you could learn.

FRANKENSTEIN: I learned. I learned. Everything will be different.

ELIZABETH: Victor.

FRANKENSTEIN: Next time.

CURTAIN

USHER

DAVID CAMPTON

Usher

*A Gothic Thriller
in Three Acts*

based on a story by
EDGAR ALLEN POE

LONDON
J. GARNET MILLER LTD

FIRST PUBLISHED BY J. GARNET MILLER LTD
IN 1973
PRINTED IN GREAT BRITAIN BY
CLARKE, DOBLE & BRENDON LIMITED, PLYMOUTH
© DAVID CAMPTON 1973

ISBN 85343 533 2

All rights reserved. An acting fee is payable on each and every performance of this play. For information regarding the fee for amateur stage performances, application should be made to the publishers:

J. Garnet Miller Ltd
10 Station Road Industrial Estate, Colwall, Malvern
Worcestershire WR13 6RN *Telephone:* 01684 540154

Australia:	Will Andrade, Box 3111, G.P.O., Sydney, N.S.W. 2001.
Kenya, Uganda and Tanganyika:	Master Play Agencies, P.O. Box 452, Nairobi, Kenya.
New Zealand:	The Play Bureau (N.Z.) Ltd., P.O. Box 3611, Wellington.
South Africa:	Darters (Pty) Ltd., P.O. Box 174, Cape Town.

Applications for all other performances should be made to: ACTAC LTD., 16 Cadogan Lane, London, S.W.1.

CAST

RODERICK USHER
MADELINE USHER
EDWIN ALLEN
LUCY
DOCTOR
OLIVER
FINN

The action takes place in the House of Usher, and a distant city. The time is autumn in the early nineteenth century.

Usher was first presented at the Library Theatre, Scarborough on June 28th, 1962 with the following cast:

RODERICK USHER	*Alan Ayckbourn*
MADELINE USHER	*Elizabeth Bell*
EDWIN ALLEN	*Peter King*
LUCY	*Marie Adams*
DOCTOR	*Stanley Page*
OLIVER	*Arnold Beck*
FINN	*Richard Gill*

Directed by *David Campton*

PRODUCTION NOTE

This play was first staged with a permanent setting, which contained a rostrum 2' 6" × 2' 6" × 6'. This became as occasion demanded a seat, a tomb, or the parapet of a bridge. Scene changes were made by lighting, sound effects, and the actors bringing on essential properties.

Pauses for scene changes should be kept to a minimum so that the play is allowed to flow uninterruptedly towards the ending of the acts.

If beams of lightweight polystyrene are used, these could be allowed to crash down just before the final curtain without hurting the actors.

ACT ONE

Scene One

USHER

RODERICK *stands alone in the centre of the room. His face is covered with his hands. His hair is silver-white, and, at first sight, he appears to be an old man. When he looks up, however, his face is a young man's face. He is, in fact, in his mid-twenties.*

Slowly he raises his head, looks over his shoulder, then stares around the room as though in a nightmare. He speaks in a whisper, which sounds like an enormous sigh.

RODERICK: Fear! Will there never be an end to fear?

FINN *enters silently. He is a dumb grotesque.*

RODERICK: Finn?

FINN *bows an acknowledgement.* RODERICK *turns to face him.* FINN *points to the door.*

RODERICK: The doctor?

FINN *nods.*

RODERICK: Send him in.

FINN *goes. The* DOCTOR *enters. He is a slightly disreputable middle-aged person with a nervous giggle.*

RODERICK: My sister?

DOCTOR: Restored, sir. Quite restored. Yes—yes. Remarkable. A curious case. She's dazed, of course. Who could blame her? I'm in need of a stimulant myself . . . Well—well . . . There she lay, the image of death. Dead, I said, when I first set eyes on her. No pulse. In extremis, I said. And myself a physician of experience—none of your fairground tooth-jerkers. A physician. But I've handed bodies to the undertaker with twice the life in them your sister had. What then, though? (*He crosses himself.*) She sighs, stirs, and opens her eyes. Alive, by thunder. There'd be less amazement at the raising of Lazarus. Snuff, sir?

He offers his box to RODERICK, *who turns away hastily.*

DOCTOR: You don't. (*He sniffs a pinch.*) In need of a stimulant. Yes—yes. Catalepsy. A trance. Fantastic. But not the first time, is it? You've had experience, sir.

RODERICK (*half to himself*): There have been—experiences.

DOCTOR: It was a lucky day for you, sir, when I left the city for my health. Yes—yes. My health.

RODERICK: We had a medicine of our own. We could tell whether a man was alive or dead. While he lived, we prayed for him: when he was dead, we buried him.

He listens intently to something outside the room.

DOCTOR: My congratulations, sir. That was beyond me. I'd have signed your sister as dead. Yes—yes. Staked my reputation. But catalepsy . . . Cold as a corpse. Yet I left her only this minute, merry as a milkmaid . . . And what now, sir? What's to be done now?

RODERICK: Mmm? Let me know your fee.

DOCTOR: I was meaning the patient, sir. What's to be done about her?

RODERICK: You are the physician.

DOCTOR: I prescribe a change of air. I'm an honest man, you see. I could sell you a bottle of coloured water for its weight in guineas, but it wouldn't have the value of a change of air.

RODERICK: A pity.

DOCTOR: Now where? you say. Anywhere where there's life. She needs to live among the living. Too much temptation to brood on the next world here. Brooding does the damage, sir.

RODERICK: Are all drugs useless?

DOCTOR: Not one as potent as a change of scene.

RODERICK: And that is impossible.

DOCTOR: Impossible? Your sister needs company, sir. Music, lights, laughter. Yes—yes. Will she find them here? I'm giving you my best advice.

RODERICK: I'll pay more than it is worth.

DOCTOR: If you won't take advice, sir, why pay at all?

RODERICK: Because, fool that I am, I hoped for help . . . What was that?

DOCTOR: That? Nothing sir. Except a dead creeper at the window.

RODERICK: A bird. Singing.

DOCTOR: That's common enough. Yes—yes. Now the Lady Madeline . . .

RODERICK: That question has been answered.

DOCTOR: Has it, sir?

RODERICK: My sister will leave this house when she dies. Even then, she must leave it in spirit. Her body will lie in the vault below.

DOCTOR: That's an inhuman sentence, sir, to pass on a girl.

RODERICK: I did not pass it.

DOCTOR: Nothing to see but a desert of grey rocks. Nothing to hear but the water lapping against the walls. How can a young woman lead a normal life here, sir?

RODERICK: Normal?

DOCTOR: How can she—marry, say?

RODERICK: Marry?

DOCTOR: That's normal, sir, for an attractive young woman.

RODERICK: Haven't you understood, man? That is *why* she

must remain here. What do the tenants think of my sister? You visit their hovels. What do they say?

DOCTOR: That's not material, sir.

RODERICK: Do they say that my sister—sleeps uneasily?

DOCTOR: Superstitious clods. I wouldn't listen.

RODERICK: Even you saw her dead, then pronounced her restored.

DOCTOR: Can she help the catalepsy?

RODERICK: None of us can help what we are. Or what is to become of us. She cannot be cured.

DOCTOR: She cannot be cured in this house, I said.

RODERICK: Then she cannot be cured . . . That bird, still.

DOCTOR: I beg to differ, sir.

RODERICK: There is no argument . . . These trills! A crescendo, bursting its throat.

DOCTOR: You put me in an awkward position, sir. Yes—yes. Uncomfortable.

RODERICK: But there are no birds here.

DOCTOR: You see, sir. I made a promise to the lady.

RODERICK: That bird—where is it?

DOCTOR: I bought a caged linnet for Lady Madeline. To cheer her. It's in her room.

RODERICK: Now—silence. The song cut short. Suddenly.

DOCTOR: Sir.

RODERICK: The bird is terrified. It chirps feebly, and hops from its perch. It panics. It hurls itself against the wall of its cage, and scrabbles on the sanded floor. It beats its wings against the bars. The air is filled with the sound of fear. Fear. Fear.

DOCTOR: Sir. Sir.

RODERICK: Fluttering, beating, scratching, tearing. Stop. Stop!

DOCTOR: Please, sir. Please.

RODERICK: It's wings are breaking. (*Gives a cry of horror and disgust.*)

DOCTOR: Sir?

RODERICK: Dead.

DOCTOR: You'll be in need of medicine yourself, sir. Yes—yes. Tincture of laudanum to encourage sleep.

RODERICK: Doctor, your patient has left her room.

DOCTOR: Sleep, sir. Nature's own restorative.

RODERICK: She is walking down the gallery. You don't recognise the rustle of a woman's skirt?

DOCTOR: You'll wake refreshed as a baby. Just a touch of laudenum.

RODERICK: She has reached the first stairs. You believe I hear nothing, don't you?

DOCTOR: I hear nothing, sir. Perhaps your imagination . . . The strain . . .

RODERICK: Perhaps it is the beginning of madness. Do you know how madness begins, Doctor? Could you tell if you looked into a madman's face? Would you recognise the glare in his eyes? Examine my eyes, Doctor. Tell me what flames you see there. Do you observe damnation in me?

DOCTOR: No.

RODERICK: Your eyes are turned away. Look at me. Am I sane? Or am I out of my depth, and drowning?

DOCTOR: Laudanum's the thing, sir.

RODERICK: I am not mad?

DOCTOR: No, sir. No—no.

RODERICK: Then what I heard, I heard.

DOCTOR: I'm hard of hearing, myself, sir.

RODERICK: I heard my sister leave her room.

DOCTOR: As you say, sir.

RODERICK: And she is here now. Now.

MADELINE *enters. She is in her mid-twenties, but looks younger. She keeps her hands clasped together until the end of the scene.*

MADELINE: How far is it to the city?

RODERICK: Madeline.

MADELINE: Shall we ride through the night? I should like to ride by moonlight.

RODERICK: You have been over-excited, my dear.

The DOCTOR *moves away from him.*

MADELINE: Why, Doctor! Thank you for my linnet. Why do birds sing so? Is it because they know their lives will be short? My bird stopped singing. Will there be birds in the city?

RODERICK: I have spoken with the Doctor, too, my dear. He agrees that it will be best if you stay here quietly. As you have always done.

MADELINE: I shall dance in the city. To music.

RODERICK: Try to understand, Madeline . . .

DOCTOR: You might understand your sister, better, sir, if it weren't for the years between you.

RODERICK: Your knowledge is limited, Doctor. My sister and I are twins.

DOCTOR: Twins? But . . .

MADELINE: Roderick broods on his sins. I have never been allowed to have any. He found his sins at the University. A girl is never sent to the University. But soon . . .

RODERICK: You will not be going to the city, my dear.

MADELINE: Roderick had a friend at the University. What was the name of your friend, Roderick? I must visit him.

RODERICK: You will not be going to the city.

MADELINE: His name is Edwin. But what is his other name? I can hardly call him Edwin when we first meet.

RODERICK: You will not meet.

MADELINE: How could you forget so soon? We shall meet when I go to the city.

RODERICK (*turning on the Doctor*): Damn you for planting the idea in her head.

DOCTOR: Plant, sir? It was already there in full blossom.

RODERICK: Doctor, tell her.

DOCTOR: A cage is all very well for a bird, sir. Yes—yes. But, if you'll pardon the expression, I can't follow your reasoning.

RODERICK: Reasons? You still ask for reasons?

DOCTOR: I'm a reasonable man, sir.

RODERICK: Where is your bird, Madeline?

MADELINE: It stopped singing.

RODERICK: When did it stop singing.

MADELINE: When I held it in my hand.

RODERICK: Show your hands to the doctor, Madeline.

MADELINE: So soft. It tried to fly away, so I held it tighter. Tighter. Tighter. It stopped singing.

She opens her hands. The DOCTOR *turns with a shudder.*

RODERICK: You had better wash away the blood, my dear. The doctor will go with you. He has a syrup to make you sleep. Haven't you, Doctor?

MADELINE: Come, Doctor. Tell me more about the ladies who visited you in the city. I shall go visiting, too. Come. How long does it take to ride there?

She goes out with the DOCTOR.

RODERICK: Oh, God! Will there never be an end to this fear?

He sinks to his knees.

ACT ONE

Scene Two

USHER

RODERICK *stands looking through the window.* FINN *enters.*

RODERICK: Madeline? (*He turns and sees* FINN). Did you let my sister know that I am waiting for her?

FINN *shakes his head.*

RODERICK: Why? Was she not in her room?

FINN *shakes his head.*

RODERICK: Look for her then. She must be in the house.

FINN *shakes his head.*

RODERICK: Where could she go?

FINN *points to the horizon.*

RODERICK: This is folly. When did you see her last? An hour ago?

FINN *holds up four fingers.*

RODERICK: Four? Four hours ago. You went to her room—was it as usual?

FINN *mimes throwing things about.*

RODERICK: Disordered. Has she taken her cloak and hood?

FINN *nods.*

RODERICK: Saddle a horse. Strike for the high road. She won't have travelled far. She hasn't the money to hire a carriage.

FINN *nods.*

RODERICK: She has money? From where?

FINN *points to* RODERICK.

RODERICK: Surely it is too old a joke for fate to laugh at. Has my sister borrowed much from me?

FINN *mimes a heavy bag of money.*

RODERICK: Then you must take money, too. Follow the road to the city. She'll cling to that like a chance of salvation. If she evades you, then search. Find her and bring her back to Usher. Forget that you need food or sleep. Remind yourself every minute that she is in danger. And not only her. Not only her . . . Allen. Years ago he lodged by the Law Courts. We swore eternal friendship in those days. Ask for him. She will be asking, too. Allen. Edwin Allen. Are you frozen, man? Get ready. Go. Go.

FINN *hurries out.*

RODERICK *follows him.*

ACT ONE

Scene Three

EDWIN'S ROOMS

EDWIN *is a well-built young man, about the same age as Roderick. He stares at* MADELINE *surprised and intrigued.*

MADELINE, *in travelling cloak, glances behind her at the retreating back of the person who has just shown her in. Then she faces* EDWIN, *and smiles.*

MADELINE: You are Mr. Allen?

EDWIN: What can I . . . ?

MADELINE: Edwin? You are very handsome.

EDWIN: I beg your pardon?

MADELINE: When my brother spoke of you, I imagined you to look like my brother.

EDWIN: You have the advantage of me.

MADELINE: You stand so stiffly. Have I done wrong? I was never taught to behave. My mother died when I was born, you see. Will you teach me to behave?

EDWIN: There has been some mistake. The misfortune is entirely mine, but we have never met before.

MADELINE: No, but you knew my brother.

EDWIN: I doubt it.

MADELINE: He said that you lived here in the city. I thought I should only have to find you and you would help me. You were friends.

EDWIN: I'm sorry. What was your brother's name?

MADELINE: Roderick.

EDWIN: Roderick?

MADELINE: My name is Madeline. My father's name was Usher.

EDWIN: Usher? I . . .

MADELINE: Roderick knew you at the University.

EDWIN: Usher! But this is incredible.

MADELINE: You remember him?

EDWIN: Where does he live?

MADELINE: Two days away. Over the hills.

EDWIN: Then it must be . . . You must be . . . Oh, my dear lady, my apologies. Friends! In those days we were like brothers. We dressed alike, talked alike, thought alike . . . And you are his sister . . . Of course I know your brother. Time was when we vowed that nothing in this life could part us. Then he was called away. Your father died, I believe.

MADELINE: Yes he—died.

EDWIN: Roderick went back to a house at the other end of the earth, and then—silence. Even I forgot. Please forgive me. What a welcome this must have seemed. But I never dreamed . . . Your brother insisted that you were confined to the house.

MADELINE: I have been ill, they say. But I am at liberty now. In the city. I can see it from your window. Waiting for me. Crowds and spires, bells and carriage wheels, scented trees and dust.

EDWIN: I apologise for the state of the room. A bachelor isn't the tidiest of creatures. These quarters are only temporary, though. In a few months I shall be married.

MADELINE: That will be a pleasant experience?

EDWIN: Bliss.

MADELINE: Then I must be married, too.

EDWIN: No doubt you will. Roderick never once said that you were beautiful. For you there will be no obstacles. What shall your husband be—general, admiral, bishop, or judge?

MADELINE: I like *you*, Edwin.

EDWIN: The choice is limited to free men.

MADELINE: I still like you, Edwin.

EDWIN: You must call on Lucy. She's a sweet girl. I should be so glad if you could be friends—Lucy and Roderick's sister.

MADELINE: Is she beautiful?

EDWIN: We love each other. Or shall I bring Lucy to call upon you? Where are you now?

MADELINE: Here.

EDWIN: Where do you live?

MADELINE: Nowhere.

EDWIN: Nowhere?

MADELINE: But look from your window. There are houses. Hundreds. There must be some place for me.

EDWIN: There are places and places.

MADELINE: I want to try them all.

EDWIN: I'm sure your brother would not thank me for letting you drift into a thieves' kitchen.

MADELINE: A thieves' kitchen. Shall I find one?

EDWIN: Not if I can help it.

MADELINE: Perhaps I should buy a house.

EDWIN: Buy?

MADELINE: People buy what they want, don't they?

EDWIN: With money.

MADELINE: I have money.

She produces a leather bag from under her cloak.

MADELINE: This is money. Round golden things.

She hands the bag to EDWIN. *He feels it, looks inside, then stares at her, astonished.*

MADELINE: On the journey, men would do anything for one of these. I gave one to a farmer for a jug of milk. He grovelled in the dust and kissed my feet.

EDWIN: A gold piece for a jug of milk.

MADELINE: I was thirsty.

EDWIN (*handing the bag to her*): Hundreds. Do you know how much?

MADELINE: I have never used money before. There was no need of it.

EDWIN: This is horrifying. You walked the streets holding a fortune. Where are your servants? Where is your luggage? Also nowhere? What was your brother thinking to send you out inviting disaster?

MADELINE: My brother is not well. But there is nothing to fear. I have money, and money can buy anything.

EDWIN: This is a fine responsibility for me. Scavengers and birds may live in style with no roofs over their heads, but you are the sister of a friend.

MADELINE: Not the *sister* of a friend. A friend.

EDWIN: A friend then. And you aren't even aware of the problem. A splendid reputation I shall have when word gets around that I have installed a young lady in lodgings. Thank heavens Lucy is understanding . . . Wait now! That may be the answer. Lucy may help.

MADELINE: So it is arranged. How clever you are.

EDWIN: Not quite arranged. There are a few hurdles yet.

MADELINE: But we are to be friends? Edwin?

EDWIN: Friends. Madeline.

MADELINE: I am glad. There is so much that you can do for me.

EDWIN: Yes. Perhaps. Yes. Now, come along to Lucy.

ACT ONE

Scene Four

Lucy's House

Lucy is younger than either Madeline or Edwin. She is a pleasant girl, shrewd enough to know the world, and practical enough to keep her corner of it tidy.

Madeline stares at Lucy like a child making up its mind about a stranger.

Edwin is just finishing a breathless, semi-comprehensible explanation.

EDWIN: . . . so why tax my brain when I could bring the problem to you? She advances into the unknown with only my name for her luggage.

LUCY: Weren't you afraid? Highway robbers lurk on the fringe of Town—one poor wretch is to be hanged tomorrow—and we still hear tales of wolves. I should have been terrified.

EDWIN: She's travel-worn, too. And I am useless. You will help, won't you?

LUCY: Did you imagine I would not?

EDWIN: There. What did I tell you? Now we must be practical.

LUCY: But what a strange way to travel—without attendance or baggage.

MADELINE: I have money.

LUCY: There is a limit to what it will buy. Oh, we shall visit the shops—at least they can provide clothes and necessities. And until tomorrow, you may borrow anything that I have. But lodgings . . . What lodgings can be found for a single unprotected girl?

EDWIN: That is the problem I put to you.

LUCY: We must consider proprieties. Madeline cannot be left to herself.

EDWIN: Then what is to be done?

LUCY: I suppose she must stay here. Yes, I shall arrange it with Mama. You shall have the room next to mine, Madeline. I am afraid until it is ready, you must sleep with me. Do you mind?

MADELINE *crosses to* LUCY *and holds her hands.*

MADELINE: How good you are. In the chapel at Usher hangs a picture of a saint. When I was little, I would gaze at her for hours. Your face is like hers—gentle, with a glow around it.

LUCY: Why, thank you.

MADELINE: She is being eaten by lions.

EDWIN: And you are friends. Splendid.

MADELINE: I never had a sister. I should like to think of you as a sister, Lucy.

LUCY: If it pleases you.

MADELINE: There is so much that you can teach me. How wise of Edwin to bring me to you. But he is clever. And brave. And strong. I shall never have anything to fear when he is taking care of me.

LUCY: I am satisfied with my bargain. But he has a few faults. We shall correct them when we are married.

MADELINE: I think he is perfect.

LUCY: You should temper your enthusiasm, my dear.

EDWIN: We must arrange a programme. Imagine—Madeline has never been to Town before. She must see everything. The theatre.

MADELINE: The Market.

LUCY: The Country Rooms.

MADELINE: And the harbour. Edwin must take me to see the ships.

LUCY: And the Zoological gardens. Edwin must take us both to see the peacocks.

MADELINE: And the hanging.

LUCY: The hanging?

MADELINE: You said that a man was to be hanged tomorrow. I have never seen a man hanged.

LUCY: Nor I. Nor do I wish to.

MADELINE: Will you take me to the hanging, Edwin?

EDWIN: Don't forget the ball. There is to be a Grand Assembly on Friday week. Do you dance, Madeline?

MADELINE: Dance? Oh, yes. Yes I want so much to dance. Will you come to the dance, Lucy?

LUCY: It has already been arranged. You shall join our party. My cousin Oliver shall partner you. He is an officer in the Militia.

MADELINE: A soldier?

LUCY: Very handsome they say.

MADELINE: Has he killed many men?

LUCY: No, but he is very fierce on manœuvres. You will just have time to visit a dressmaker. I can already see you conquering the regiment, Madeline.

MADELINE: Yes. It will be a battle indeed.

EDWIN: Capital! What other excursions can we plan together? We must show you all the sights along the river—the Castle, the Exchange . . . We must explore everything. I can hardly wait.

MADELINE: I cannot wait at all. Will you take me to the river now?

EDWIN: Now? But your journey . . . You must rest. Tomorrow . . .

MADELINE: Don't say impossible. Nothing is impossible to you. Dear Edwin. You are so resourceful. Come now. Come.

EDWIN: But, Madeline . . . If you insist. Will you come with us, Lucy? . . . Lucy?

LUCY *watches them go, then slowly walks after them.*

ACT ONE

Scene Five

A BRIDGE

FINN *stands alone, looking about him. He withdraws into the shadows.*

EDWIN *and* MADELINE *enter.* EDWIN *carries a walking stick.*

EDWIN (*Pointing with the stick*): . . . and there, the Castle defying time and sieges for six hundred years. Rather impressive at sunset, eh? But we'd better turn back. You must be home before dusk. In the city nocturnal animals aren't as friendly as your foxes and stoats.

MADELINE: Stay on the bridge. (*She peers over.*) Look at the black river underneath. I wish I were a fish in it, to feel the darkness flowing by me. Do drowned men feel it? Can they battle with currents, and race with the tide? I can taste the salt wind on my lips. (*She jumps up on to the parapet.*) I want to be strong and feel like the river. I want to embrace the sea.

EDWIN: Let me help you down . . . The sun is sinking. Lucy will be thinking you *have* been swallowed by the river.

MADELINE: The shadows are mingling with the dusk. It reminds me of Usher. Yes, let us go back to Lucy.

They turn, walk a few steps along the bridge, and are met by FINN, *who stands in their way.*

EDWIN: I beg your pardon.

FINN *does not move.*

EDWIN: Sir?

FINN *neither moves nor replies.* EDWIN *shrugs his shoulders as at a village idiot, and steps aside. He is about to walk forward, when* FINN *blocks his way again.*

EDWIN: You require the entire path? At any other time, I'd dispute it. However, this once . . . Pass—friend!

He draws aside with MADELINE, *and waves* FINN *on.*

EDWIN: But keep in mind that my companion, not my inclination saves you from a broken head.

FINN *does not move.*

EDWIN: Immovable, sir? You have the right of way, what more do you want?

FINN *points to* MADELINE.

EDWIN: Damn your insolence. (*He pushes* FINN *back at the point of his stick.*) Stand aside, lout. You offend the lady. Have you seen him before?

MADELINE: Never.

His arm around MADELINE, EDWIN *walks by* FINN. FINN *pulls* MADELINE *towards him. She gives a tiny scream.*

EDWIN: Would you?

He knocks down FINN's *arm with his stick.* MADELINE *draws away.*

EDWIN: Ask for a sore back, and you shall have it.

He raises his stick, but FINN *catches his wrist.* EDWIN *holds* FINN's *arm, trying to force him to give way.*

Casually, with his free hand, FINN *takes the stick from* EDWIN. *He runs his hand approvingly along it, as though admiring its qualities. Then he smiles, bows, and hands the stick back to* EDWIN.

EDWIN *takes it astounded.*

FINN *bows again, and walks away.*

MADELINE: I'm cold.

EDWIN: There's—nothing to fear. I'm with you.

They walk away.

ACT ONE

Scene Six

USHER

RODERICK'S VOICE (*in the darkness*): Finn. Finn. Are there no clocks in the city?

RODERICK *stands in a small circle of light.*

RODERICK: Have you lost count of time? Is she invisible, or are you blind? She could never lie hidden so long, even in Babylon. She is beautiful as bright poison. Let a man be tempted, and . . . Better for her to die first. There must be no more breeding. Let the line die out. God, let the Ushers die with me.

The light fades.

RODERICK'S VOICE (*in the darkness*): Bring her back man. Now. Bring her back or let her die.

ACT ONE

Scene Seven

THE ASSEMBLY ROOMS

The strains of a waltz can be heard in the distance.

LUCY *is sitting with* OLIVER, *a fatuous young man in dress uniform.*

OLIVER: I say, you've picked a deuced lonely corner to sit in, Cousin.

LUCY: If I must sit alone, I would rather be unobserved.

OLIVER: Dash it, you're not alone. I'm with you.

LUCY: Yes, Oliver. But where is your partner?

OLIVER: Waltzing with *your* partner. She's a charmer, eh?

LUCY: She has a pretty face.

OLIVER: More than that.

LUCY: What—more?

OLIVER: Deuced difficult to explain. Never was good at words. Couldn't talk to *her*, you know. Told her that it was deuced hot for the time of year, and that she was a deuced fine girl. What else was there to say? But she's a charmer. Mysterious.

The waltz ends.

LUCY: Sometimes I find her terrifying.

OLIVER: She's not like you, coz. You're as deuced plain-spoken as a fellow.

LUCY: Which puts me at a deuced disadvantage.

OLIVER: Can't see that. You're getting married.

LUCY: You said that a man liked mystery.

OLIVER: Not in a wife. Like to know what a wife's thinking about.

LUCY: Thank you for your reassurance, Oliver. Edwin . . .

OLIVER: Deuced faithful—Edwin. Wouldn't look at another woman. And I'd call him out if he did.

MADELINE's *laugh is heard off.*

LUCY: Here they come.

MADELINE *enters with* EDWIN. *She is still laughing.*

EDWIN: Never tell me again you were taught nothing in the country. You whirled in my arms like a snowflake. Where did you learn to waltz?

MADELINE: From the snowflakes . . . Why didn't you join us, Lucy?

LUCY: Mama believes the waltz is an immodest dance.

MADELINE: What does that mean?

EDWIN: It means we enjoy it too much.

OLIVER: I say, Miss Usher . . . I say . . . Deuced fine music, eh?

MADELINE: It sparkles like fountains among the lights.

OLIVER: Yes. Deuced fine band.

MADELINE: Why did it end so soon?

EDWIN: The other dancers don't have your stamina.

MADELINE: Oh, the lights. The lights.

LUCY: Have you strength left for the quadrille, Edwin? You promised.

EDWIN: Yours to command, my dear.

MADELINE: The lights . . .

LUCY: Not command, Edwin . . . Is Oliver to partner you, Madeline?

EDWIN *takes* LUCY *towards the door.*

MADELINE (*staring at vacancy*): Lights. Lights. Lights.

EDWIN: Madeline! Are you ill?

MADELINE: Lights. Li . . . Li . . .

EDWIN: Madeline!

He runs forward and catches her as she sways.

LUCY: Oh no!

OLIVER: I say . . . I say.

EDWIN: Oliver!

OLIVER: Yes, of course.

Together they support MADELINE *to the seat.* EDWIN *sits next to her, supporting her.*

OLIVER: Deuced sudden.

MADELINE *opens her eyes.*

EDWIN: A touch of giddiness. Oliver, dear fellow, open the window.

OLIVER: It *is* open. Why not walk on the lawn? Fresh air. Better than burned feathers.

MADELINE: It was—nothing. I shall sit here for a while, where it is cool. Stay with me, Edwin. Was I . . . ? Did I keep you long from the dance?

LUCY: The set for the quadrille is not yet complete.

MADELINE: Then you must not miss it.

LUCY: My dear, you have my partner . . . I'm sorry. That was less than generous.

OLIVER: Don't fret, coz. I'll partner you.

LUCY: Thank you, Oliver, but . . .

She turns to speak to EDWIN, *but he is occupied with* MADELINE.

EDWIN: Your hands are like marble.

LUCY *turns, and walks away with* OLIVER.

MADELINE: Will you warm them for me?

EDWIN: A compromising picture. I must ask leave of Lucy.

He turns, just in time to see her go. He rises.

Slowly EDWIN *sits.*

MADELINE: Don't fret. She will always forgive you—again and again. But you are alone with me. The first time since we walked by the river.

Music begins.

MADELINE: Edwin—I am afraid.

EDWIN: Have I misjudged you? I thought your courage put lions to shame.

MADELINE: Believe me, Edwin. Try to believe me.

EDWIN: Why shouldn't I?

MADELINE: Because once I lied to you. That evening by the river. You remember the man who accosted us? You asked if I had seen him before.

EDWIN: And *have* you been consorting with monsters?

MADELINE: His name is Finn. He is my brother's servant.

EDWIN: Why that explains . . . But if he is your servant, why make such a mystery?

MADELINE: Not *my* servant. My brother's. Now you understand why you must help me.

EDWIN: I am completely bewildered.

MADELINE: Since that moment, he has never been far from me. The first night I shared Lucy's bed, I woke while the moonlight streamed through the window. It cast a shadow on the wall. His face was at the window.

EDWIN: What does this Peeping Tom want with you?

MADELINE: He has been ordered to carry me back to Usher.

EDWIN: By whom?

MADELINE: By my brother—who else?

EDWIN: What a topsy-turvy world you live in. You say that Roderick arranged for your abduction on the very day that you arrived here.

MADELINE: Is that so incredible?

EDWIN: It is when he has just been put to the expense of sending you.

MADELINE: He did not send me. I escaped. Do you know what a prison is like? No light—only shadows. No laughter—only whispers. No living—only waiting for death. And Usher is worse than any prison. So I robbed my brother, and ran away. The money you saw. It was stolen. The man who was hanged last week stole less. I could be hanged too, couldn't I? But I would rather—rather die on a gallows than go back to Usher.

EDWIN: Calm yourself, Madeline.

MADELINE: You think I am still lying.

EDWIN: You mustn't let your imagination race. I knew Roderick. We were friends.

MADELINE: Finn is waiting. He knows that, sooner or later, he will find me unprotected, and I shall become a prisoner again. Next time, the doors will be thicker, the bolts heavier. And will you let it happen. You will let it happen, and I am lost. Lost. I had to grab. Understand now why. There was no time. No time for the game the ladies play.

EDWIN: I'll fetch a glass of negus. Revive you.

MADELINE: Stay with me, Edwin.

EDWIN: There's nothing to tremble at. I'll hurry back.

MADELINE: Hold me.

EDWIN: Your shawl . . .

He arranges her shawl. She grasps his arms.

MADELINE: Hold me. Hold tightly.

EDWIN: I'd no idea such slender fingers had so much strength in them.

MADELINE: I had a singing bird once, but he could not bear me to hold him tightly. Closer, Edwin.

EDWIN: I am to marry Lucy. Remember? Do you want to hurt her? Please.

He detaches himself.

MADELINE: When I am gone . . .

EDWIN: These are mere nightmares.

MADELINE: Don't let them bury me alive again.

EDWIN: Sit quietly until I return. The wine will restore you.

MADELINE: Promise.

EDWIN: Very well. I promise. If the creature spirits you away, I shall gallop on my white horse to snatch you from his clutches.

MADELINE: Remember that.

EDWIN *goes.*

The music ends.

MADELINE *puts her hands to her head. Then she stands up, and looks about her wildly. Her shawl slips from her shoulders. Holding it in one hand, and trailing it behind her, she goes to the window. She pauses there, and the shawl drops from her hand. She backs from the window.* FINN *follows her in. She stands staring at him, swaying slightly, as though hypnotised.* FINN *grabs her arm. She goes limp. He catches her before she falls. He carries her out through the window, but leaves her shawl.*

EDWIN *returns with a glass of wine. He glances around the room.*

EDWIN: Madeline?

He goes to the window, and looks out.

EDWIN (*calling softly*): Madeline.

He turns back to the room, and sees the shawl lying on the floor. He picks it up.

EDWIN (*in a whisper*): Madeline!

He hurries to the entrance where he meets LUCY *returning with* OLIVER.

EDWIN: Madeline. Where is she?

OLIVER: Deuced silly question. Left her with you.

EDWIN: I left her to fetch this. (*He thrusts the glass at* OLIVER, *who takes it obediently*.) Did you notice her in the ballroom?

OLIVER: Can't say I did.

LUCY: But why the mystery? Surely Madeline can walk from a room without the watch being called.

EDWIN: She can walk, but should she vanish?

LUCY: She could have ventured on to the lawn.

EDWIN: Into the night air, wearing dancing slippers, and leaving her shawl behind? I didn't believe her. What if she told the truth?

OLIVER: Don't lash yourself into a lather. I'll take a walk outside. She can't be far away.

EDWIN: Even if she has been abducted?

LUCY: Edwin!

OLIVER: You have a deuced gory imagination.

EDWIN: Haven't you?

OLIVER: No imagination at all. Don't pay in the Army. (*Suddenly realises that he is holding the glass.*) What shall I do with this?

EDWIN: Drink it.

OLIVER: Oh. (*Takes a mouthful.*) Deuced good. We'll be back in less time than it takes to slope arms. (*Calls tentatively through the window.*) Miss Usher . . . That is unless . . . (*He chuckles.*) I say, Miss Usher . . .

He wanders out through the window still clutching the glass.

EDWIN: And if they are not back?

LUCY: If is a big word for two letters.

EDWIN: How can you keep so calm?

LUCY: I have so little notion of what is supposed to have happened.

EDWIN: She told me a fantastic tale of her brother. Who would have accepted it? But if it were true . . . I made a promise.

LUCY: To follow her to Usher?

EDWIN: How did you guess?

LUCY: Don't go, Edwin.

EDWIN: Why?

LUCY: I—I feel that you will be in—some danger there.

EDWIN: From Roderick? I'll trust our friendship still has a meaning.

LUCY: I was not thinking of Roderick Usher.

EDWIN: Madeline?

LUCY: I cannot struggle against my own nature. Who said that I was perfect? Do I count for less than her.

EDWIN: If only half she told me were true, she needs me desperately.

LUCY: Don't follow her to Usher, Edwin.

EDWIN: You want me to break my word?

LUCY: It is done every day in so many ways. I would rather keep you with feet of clay than lose you.

EDWIN: Who spoke of losing? You have my promise too, Lucy . . . But what zanies we are, for all we know she is crossing the lawn this minute on the arm of Oliver.

OLIVER comes in through the window. He holds out an object to EDWIN. EDWIN takes it.

EDWIN: Her slipper.

CURTAIN

ACT TWO

Scene One

USHER

Sunset. RODERICK faces FINN.

RODERICK: He is here.

FINN nods.

RODERICK: Then we have no choice but to admit him.

FINN mimes cutting a throat.

RODERICK: No, Finn. However simple. The young man must be given the dues of friendship. Let us hope that he respects them. Show him in.

FINN withdraws.

RODERICK takes a few paces towards the door, then turns back. He faces the window, but winces as the sunlight strikes his eyes. He covers his eyes with one hand. He stiffens as he hears footsteps outside.

EDWIN strides into the room, trying to hide his nervousness with a show of authority.

EDWIN: Was that gargoyle ordered to deceive me? Where is Roderick Usher?

RODERICK: Yours to command, Edwin.

He turns.

EDWIN: Roderick!

RODERICK: My hair? Snow in summer. I put on white when my father died.

EDWIN: We—haven't seen each other since . . . Your father died unexpectedly.

RODERICK: He hanged himself in front of this window. The setting sun was the last light he saw. He left a message to say that he could not endure another night in this house.

EDWIN: I—I was never told.

RODERICK: I'm a bad correspondent. Besides, he left so much unfinished business . . . But this is a cold greeting for you, Edwin. Welcome. Welcome to Usher. A fire has been burning in your room since morning.

EDWIN: You knew that I was coming?

RODERICK: Our entertainment has grown somewhat rusty. Visitors seldom call. Perhaps the atmosphere is too chill for them. The fault of building by a lake. My forefathers have a lot to answer for . . . How did I—? What is more natural than a visit to a friend after all these years.

EDWIN: You knew that I was following Madeline.

RODERICK: You must be exhausted after two days of crooked lanes and broken tracks. Do you wonder that I stagnate rather than face them?

EDWIN: Where is she?

RODERICK: In her room . . . But you shall see over the house tomorrow. It has a romantic charm, best observed by daylight.

EDWIN: May I see her?

RODERICK: Parts of the building have fallen into disrepair. In fact I advise you to keep to your room after dusk. If there is anything you need you have only to ring, and Finn will attend you. You will find candles enough to last until daylight.

EDWIN: When may I see her?

RODERICK: Madeline? . . . When you return, you must thank your fiancée for taking such care of her. Some day we must repay her.

EDWIN: When shall I see Madeline?

RODERICK: Soon. Tomorrow. Or the day after. Very soon.

EDWIN: Now. Take me to her now.

RODERICK: An order, Edwin?

EDWIN: This minute. I insist.

RODERICK: Impossible.

EDWIN: Ah!

RODERICK: She is asleep . . . Finn has instructions to serve supper in your room. You must be exhausted.

EDWIN (*shouting*): My patience is!

RODERICK (*his hands over his ears*): Your voice!

EDWIN: I want the truth. No more tricks, lies or evasions. The truth!

RODERICK: No more. No more.

EDWIN: What have you done to Madeline.

RODERICK: Torment. Torment.

EDWIN (*shaking Roderick*): Where is she?

RODERICK (*himself screaming now*): Enough.

EDWIN *releases him. Pause.* RODERICK *trembles violently, and murmurs confusedly.*

RODERICK: Don't . . . Don't ever . . .

EDWIN (*ashamed*): You provoked me.

RODERICK: My ears. Knives. Knives.

EDWIN: Now you make me into a boor.

RODERICK: I suffer from . . . How can I explain?

EDWIN: I apologise.

RODERICK: A curious malady. Delusion maybe, but it grows sharper with the years. A morbid acuteness of the senses. Do you understand? Light and colour dazzle my eyes. The most delicate perfume chokes me. To you my food would be a tasteless mash. And my hearing . . .

EDWIN: Why do you hedge me?

RODERICK: Deafness would come as a relief. Can you hear the scattering of mice? the avalanche of the white owl and the death scream of his victim? If only I could stop my ears.

EDWIN: Madeline disappeared.

RODERICK: Madeline? That was an unpardonable touch of melodrama.

EDWIN: Can you quiet my suspicions?

RODERICK: I can remember a season when there would have been no suspicions.

EDWIN: Times change.

RODERICK: There's an evil magic in the calendar—I have been bewitched into a monster, and you, my accuser.

EDWIN: I am not accusing . . .

RODERICK: What depravity do you suspect? What are my secret vices? Or are they unmentionable? You had no inkling of them—how many centuries ago?

EDWIN: You are trying to confuse me. What has our friendship to do with Madeline?

RODERICK: I need a friend. Now more than ever. My dear Edwin, trust me. At least until morning. See then how much remains of the mystery.

EDWIN: I—I . . .

RODERICK: Madeline is safe and well. Would you have me drag her from her bed to satisfy your curiosity? You have my word. There is nothing to fear.

EDWIN: Nothing?

RODERICK: Nothing.

A rumble as the house trembles.

EDWIN: What was that?

RODERICK: Only the house.

The tremor is repeated.

RODERICK: My ancestors built on infirm foundations. But it will last my lifetime.

FINN *enters.*

RODERICK: Finn will lead you upstairs. He has a candle to light you to bed.

EDWIN: Thank you.

RODERICK: Goodnight . . . Edwin . . . We are still friends?

EDWIN: Still.

RODERICK: Remember me in your prayers. Sleep well.

EDWIN *and* FINN *go out.*

RODERICK (*with a small bitter laugh*): Sleep!

The house rumbles.

RODERICK *turns to face the window, looking up to the top of the frame. He holds out his hand.*

RODERICK: Do you sleep?

He turns and stumbles from the room.

ACT TWO

Scene Two

USHER

Moonlight glimmers on MADELINE *standing by the window. She is in white, and her feet are bare. She is listening, and waiting. Suddenly she darts into the shadows.*

EDWIN *enters with a candle. He stumbles, and tries to peer into the darkness. He has almost passed* MADELINE *when she takes his arm.*

He turns with a smothered cry.

EDWIN: Madeline! Are you safe? What happ . . .

She puts her hand over his mouth.

MADELINE: Sssh!

EDWIN: What have they done to you?

MADELINE: Follow me.

EDWIN: Where?

MADELINE: Don't be afraid. I shall be with you.

EDWIN: But . . .

MADELINE: Don't speak. Just hold my hand.

She leads him away. They are barely out of sight when FINN *emerges from the shadow. He looks after them, then hurries away in the opposite direction.*

ACT TWO

Scene Three

THE VAULTS

Darkness. EDWIN *and* MADELINE *enter.* EDWIN *is still holding the candle. He stops suddenly, and splutters.*

EDWIN: Something brushed against my mouth. It felt like a cobweb. Where are we?

MADELINE: The vaults. Tunnels, alcoves, and cells.

EDWIN *puts down his candle on a slab. Something about the shape strikes him as familiar.*

MADELINE: The house is built upon catacombs.

EDWIN: Surely this is . . .

MADELINE: The main burial chamber is over there—just beyond us. In the days of the castle these were dungeons. There are still bones in some of the alcoves. You are not worried by dry bones, are you?

EDWIN: Why have we come here?

MADELINE: Roderick will not follow us. He hates this place. When we were children, I played a game on him. I chained him to the wall—some of the cells are still provided with staples, and left him. He had screamed himself dumb by the time he was rescued.

EDWIN: What a horrible child you must have been.

MADELINE: He was afraid. He has always been afraid. That is why he tried to keep me from you. But I escaped, and you searched for me. Now we are together. Here. Even here. (*Holds out her arms to him.*) Come to me.

EDWIN *takes a step towards her. The house rumbles.*

MADELINE: What holds you back?

EDWIN: That noise . . .

MADELINE: Only the house, creaking.

EDWIN: It sounds worse down here.

MADELINE: Some of the passages crawl under the lake. Water oozes down the walls in green trails. And there—do you see?—the fissure.

EDWIN: The fissure?

MADELINE: The crack. It stretches from the roof to the foundations. Every year it opens a little wider. One day this place will split, and crumble into the tarn.

EDWIN: A merry prospect.

MADELINE: Nothing lasts for ever. Everyone must die. Take me into your arms, Edwin.

EDWIN: In this charnel house?

MADELINE: My family lies in there. Do they trouble you? I would show them to you, but the door creaks. Even Roderick would brave the cellars if he heard the door creak. One day I shall lie with them. My coffin is waiting for me. Your face is very pale in the candlelight Edwin.

EDWIN: Your—coffin?

MADELINE: It is lined with silk and the pillow is edged with lace. Soft and smooth. Death must be a remarkable experience. What a disappointment if it were not—being so final. That is why it is so important to live while we may. I wonder—what is the taste of death? Bitter, I should think. But I want to know the taste of love first, Edwin . . .

EDWIN: Have you forgotten Lucy?

MADELINE: Tell me what she looks like. What colour are her eyes? Look at me and tell me what she looks like.

EDWIN: I kept my promise. I followed you here. You are safe. Now come away.

MADELINE: Wait. (*She picks up something from the ground.*)

EDWIN: Why?

MADELINE: Here. (*She thrusts the object at him.*)

EDWIN: What . . . ? (*He takes the thing, but gives a gasp of disgust on realising that it is a skull.*)

MADELINE: Only a skull.

EDWIN (*thrusting it back at her*): Take it. Take it.

MADELINE: There are more of them in the corners. I played with them as a child. They were all men once like you.

EDWIN: You make my flesh crawl.

MADELINE: Look at it. Once it had eyes like yours. Once it had lips like yours. Think, Edwin. When you are rolled in a dusty corner too, you will have lost the chance to love. If you must remember, remember that.

With a cry, he hurls the skull from him. There is a pause as he stands, trembling, wiping his hands. MADELINE *goes to him, but his back is turned to her.*

MADELINE: It's so dark.

EDWIN: So cold.

She touches his arm, but he moves away.

MADELINE: My hands are warm. Feel.

She puts her hand against his. He holds it. She caresses his arm with her other hand.

MADELINE: We are alive, you and I. Both alive. Can you feel my heart? (*She rests her cheek against his shoulders.*) Look at me, Edwin. Won't you look at me? What face do you see now as you stare into the darkness. Hers? Mine?—His?

EDWIN (*swinging round to face her.*) You—you . . .

MADELINE: Yes, Edwin?

EDWIN (*grasping her arms, and shaking her*): You—wild thing.

MADELINE: You are bruising my arms.

EDWIN: You *are* dangerous.

MADELINE: A gentle touch would hold me.

EDWIN: With your blazing eyes.

MADELINE: Gently. Like this.

She puts her arms around his neck, and draws his lips to hers.

MADELINE: Is that love?

EDWIN: I don't know. Whatever it is turns my brain to fire, and my will to water.

MADELINE: You won't leave me here?

EDWIN: Never.

MADELINE: You'll take me away?

EDWIN: To the end of the earth.

He kisses her.

RODERICK: Cock-crow already?

MADELINE *and* EDWIN *part.* RODERICK *walks into the light.*

RODERICK: I had no idea, Edwin, that you were so eager to explore my house.

MADELINE *draws closer to* EDWIN. *He puts a protective arm around her.*

RODERICK: I thought you would have preferred to wait until morning. Especially after my warning.

EDWIN: Danger comes from any direction.

RODERICK: That is why, if you must investigate the underworld, you need a reliable guide.

EDWIN: I trust Madeline.

RODERICK: Madeline is ill.

MADELINE: I am not.

RODERICK: Your appearance, my dear. Your actions. What must Edwin think?

MADELINE: Don't listen to him. He wants to part us.

RODERICK: The doctor will treat you tomorrow.

MADELINE: The doctor makes me ill. After his medicines I cannot stay awake.

RODERICK: Take her to her room.

FINN *appears*.

MADELINE: Finn?

RODERICK: This time, when he bolts the door, he will make sure that you are inside.

EDWIN: If Madeline needs any assistance. I can give it.

RODERICK: Thank you, but no. It had better be Finn. He is enormously strong. Only he can restrain her.

MADELINE: Perhaps you had better tell Edwin of my other sports. Tell him that I walk through bolted doors. I drink hemlock, and ride on a broomstick. Tell him that I fly to the moon on Hallowe'en.

RODERICK: Take her away.

EDWIN *stands in front of* MADELINE.

EDWIN: Pass me first.

Slowly FINN *walks over to* EDWIN.

MADELINE: No. I'll go. There'll be another day tomorrow. And you won't forget.

She lets FINN *lead her away.*

EDWIN: What devilry is this?

RODERICK: I know little of the rules of hospitality. Would it be a breach to ask a guest to leave so soon?

EDWIN: When I leave, she will leave with me.

RODERICK: Madeline is my charge. Your thoughts belong with Lucy. You are to marry her—remember?

EDWIN: What of Madeline?

RODERICK: Charming girl, eh? The wedding will be soon?

EDWIN: Where will *she* marry?

RODERICK: God bless you both.

EDWIN: Is she to love shadows?

RODERICK: Usher ladies never marry.

EDWIN: And that is Madeline's future—a preserved flower, to be pressed in full bloom. And for what? So the sacred Usher line can be kept pure.

RODERICK: So that it can be snuffed out. I hate my name. I cursed my father that he gave it to me. Do you know what the name of Usher means? Damnation. There lie my ancestors—an anthology of corruption. Choose any crime in the calendar; name any beastliness that makes men worse than beasts—murder, incest, suicide, lycanthropy, necrophilia—you will find them all catalogued in there. All Ushers. Madness flows in the sap of my family tree, and in every generation, bursts forth into strange and horrible flower. That is why Madeline must be confined. Her blood is infected like mine.

EDWIN: Delusions.

RODERICK: A sign?

EDWIN: You are as sane as I am.

RODERICK: Not one of the line has escaped the curse. If the blow has not yet fallen, it is still to come. And it will come . . . I am not mad, you said?

EDWIN: Of course not.

RODERICK: Bless you.

EDWIN: But you are driving yourself to it.

RODERICK: The shadow drives me.

EDWIN: Shadow?

RODERICK: The fear.

EDWIN: Fight it.

RODERICK: With what?

EDWIN: Hope.

RODERICK: There is no hope. Sentence has been pronounced.

EDWIN: Fear is only a state of mind.

RODERICK: Oh, no. Fear haunts this house. It was built into the very stones. It lurks beyond the candleflame. It whispers down the corridors. It lies by your bed.

EDWIN: Fear of what?

RODERICK: Just fear. Purposeless fear. Fear of living. Fear of dying. Fear of night. Fear of day. Fear of enemies. Fear of friends. Fear of the future. Fear of the past. Fear. Fear. Fear.

EDWIN: Hysteria.

RODERICK: Fear.

EDWIN: It *will* drive you mad if you give way.

RODERICK: It comes to each of us. Each Usher.

EDWIN: That is why Madeline must be taken from this place.

RODERICK: Madeline?

EDWIN: Before she is affected.

RODERICK: Madeline . . . Clinging in your arms. Her lips pressed to yours. Madeline. (*Pulls himself together. Briskly.*) Did I break the spell?

EDWIN: You—broke the spell.

RODERICK: And you. What will you do now?

EDWIN: Have patience until she is able to leave.

RODERICK: A friendly gesture.

EDWIN: We are still friends.

RODERICK: It would be a friendly act to lead a friend to safety.

EDWIN: What do you mean?

RODERICK: These vaults now. They are unhealthy. Fit for only slime and beetles. Light and air are much better for you. Dear fellow, I must bring you to the light and air. And if you will not come with me, I must bring the light and air to you. Yes, I must bring the light and air to you.

He picks up the candle, and leads EDWIN *out.*

ACT TWO

Scene Four

USHER

LUCY, *wearing a travelling cloak, stands alone. She looks about her, then goes to the window* . . . RODERICK *enters silently.*

RODERICK: Welcome, dear lady.

LUCY *turns with a little cry of surprise.*

RODERICK: I am Roderick Usher. I am so grateful that you accepted my invitation.

LUCY: *Your* invitation?

RODERICK: I meant that I was happy to agree when Madeline suggested your visit. My sister wrote to you, of course. To have you stay is only a return of hospitality. She often speaks of you. Warmly. Very warmly . . . Allow me.

He helps her from her cloak.

LUCY: I hoped that one day I might see Usher. Madeline seemed reluctant to talk about her home. No wonder. My mother's house must have seemed a bird's nest to her after this.

FINN *enters.* RODERICK *hands the cloak to him, then dismisses him.*

RODERICK: We retain a fragment of tattered grandeur. But consider yourself at home here. It seemed an excellent idea to invite you while Edwin was staying. You are to be married soon, I understand: a most happy match. Yes, an excellent idea. When you leave, Edwin will be able to accompany you.

LUCY: You are very kind. But there is one small question that I must ask.

RODERICK: Anything, dear lady.

LUCY: Why did you send for me?

Pause.

RODERICK: Surely, I . . .

LUCY: My stay here will be bearable only if I know the truth.

Pause.

RODERICK: I would not wish anything to come between Edwin and yourself.

LUCY: Or any*one*?

RODERICK: My sister is an impulsive young woman. Edwin is a susceptible young man. An explosive mixture.

LUCY: I had a foreshadowing of it.

RODERICK: Remind him of his duty.

LUCY: If it were only a question of duty, I would not wish to hold him.

RODERICK: You love him?

LUCY: My—feelings are engaged.

RODERICK: Then fight for him.

LUCY: Fight?

RODERICK: I thought you would prefer the plain term.

LUCY: Were your motives in sending for me entirely disinterested?

RODERICK: The outcome of this adventure depends upon *your* motives. It is in your interest to bring Edwin to his senses. I pin my faith to that . . . But Finn has just announced dinner. You must meet my sister again . . .

ACT TWO

Scene Five

USHER

RODERICK, LUCY, EDWIN, *and* MADELINE. LUCY *and* MADELINE *look at each other*—LUCY *challenging,* MADELINE *defiant. Then* LUCY *turns to* EDWIN. *Uncomfortable, he looks away.*

LUCY: What a strange light. Is there a storm in the air?

Pause.

LUCY: When I was a child, I would hide at the first suspicion of thunder. Since then I have learned that storms are sometimes necessary. The air is always cleared afterwards.

Pause.

LUCY: What have you been doing since you arrived at Usher, Edwin?

Pause.

LUCY: In a mansion as fantastic as this you must have found something to catch your fancy. Madeline . . .

EDWIN *swings round to face her, but she continues smoothly.*

LUCY: If Edwin has taken a vow of silence, you must tell me everything.

Suddenly MADELINE *crosses to* EDWIN.

LUCY: At dinner you promised to guide me over the house. Will you show me now?

EDWIN: Shall I—join you?

LUCY: Not for the present, Edwin. Madeline and I will be exchanging sisterly secrets. It is so long since we had a tête-à-tête. More than a week. So much can happen in a week. Will you, Madeline?

MADELINE *leaves* EDWIN *and goes to* LUCY. *Smiling she takes her arm.*

MADELINE: Yes. Yes, I must.

She and LUCY *go out together.*

RODERICK (*pointing out through the window*): Look. The roof is alight with St. Elmo's fire. Cold blue flames over the gables. Look. Flickering corpse candles. You despise omens. Look.

EDWIN: Madeline wrote no letter.

RODERICK: Can you feel the electricity? My skin crawls and prickles.

EDWIN: You sent for Lucy.

RODERICK: Sparks crackle as they fly.

EDWIN: It was an absurd piece of deceit. Clumsy. Obvious.

RODERICK: So much the better. No explanations are necessary.

EDWIN: Unfriendly.

RODERICK: I'm alone, Edwin: alone in an empty and echoing place. The darkness crouches ready to spring upon me. Once Madeline shared my loneliness. We said our prayers together. But that is past . . . All past . . . What I did, Edwin, was to help you. You will take Lucy with you.

EDWIN: So simple!

RODERICK: Church and marriage-bed are waiting. Cradles and baby-cries. What a brood you will father. Like their parents—hard-headed, healthy, unplagued by ghosts. I envy you.

EDWIN: Envy?

RODERICK: Like Lucifer cast out.

EDOIN: You're the victim of your own imagination. You have property and position. If a crowded nursery attracts you, why don't you marry?

The house rumbles.

RODERICK: Rotten. Rotten. Threadbare tapestries and moth-eaten banners. Behind a noble façade, stairs and beams riddled with worm. The fissure crawls up the wall. The upper rooms are carpeted with dust.

EDWIN: It could all be made good.

RODERICK: It is not waiting for repairs. It is waiting to be destroyed. Ushers made this house: this house made Ushers. Don't tempt us with repairs and marriages.

EDWIN: Come back to town with me.

RODERICK: With this maggot in my brain? Alarm bells, street cries, and iron-bound wheels. The clatter alone would have me raving. What else can I do but wait here, silent with the dust?

EDWIN: Wait? For what?

RODERICK: Dear fellow, you are so distressingly sane. But haven't you ever felt the terror—on the fringe of a nightmare, say—of being at the mercy of a power beyond you? That at the raising of a finger—pouff. No? The power is there, though. It amuses them to linger, but one day the finger will be raised. Pouff. We are so helpless.

EDWIN: Superstitious nonsense. No-one can tell what the future holds.

RODERICK: But if you knew—beyond all doubt . . .

EDWIN: Whatever comes, we must face it with hope and courage.

RODERICK: Certainty destroys hope. When the noose tightens round your throat, can you still say "hope"? . . . Listen.

EDWIN: To what?

RODERICK: A cry?

EDWIN: Where?

RODERICK: No. Not a cry. It was a door opening.

EDWIN: I heard nothing.

RODERICK: Yes, a door. The burial chamber. Madeline has led Lucy into the vaults. If . . . No, that is impossible. But if she . . . I should not have let them go. If . . . No. No, no. No.

He hurries out. EDWIN *follows.*

ACT TWO

Scene Six

THE VAULTS

MADELINE *and* LUCY *enter*. MADELINE *carries a candle which she puts down on the slab.*

LUCY: ... suspicion.

MADELINE: ... and one day I shall lie there with my father and mother. My father died by his own hand. Are you afraid to die, Lucy?

LUCY: Die?

MADELINE: You are going to die, did you know that . . .? Many years ago this was a torture chamber. Before I was born.

LUCY: Now will you listen to me?

MADELINE: Now we can hear only the drip of water from the roof, but in those days, the walls echoed with screams. I wish I had lived in those days.

LUCY: Do let us talk sensibly. I said that your conduct with Edwin had not been above suspicion.

MADELINE: Oh, yes. Edwin.

LUCY: You admit it?

MADELINE: Beyond here lie the cells.

LUCY: Madeline! ... It is an unpleasant subject. Sometimes, though, unpleasantness has to be faced. This—misunderstanding had better be resolved before it becomes worse.

MADELINE: I want you to see the cells.

LUCY: And I want you to know what is in my mind. I will not be put off with further—sight-seeing.

MADELINE: I wouldn't hurt you.

LUCY: Perhaps you didn't mean to. Perhaps you didn't realise what you were doing. It is possible, I suppose, to steal a man's affections unawares—particularly when you are ignorant of his character. I know Edwin—better than he knows himself. He is incurably romantic. At first cry of distress he was bound to fly to your side. That is the charitable view.

MADELINE: Why don't you come to the cells, Lucy?

LUCY: As soon as this matter is thrashed out, we shall return to Edwin.

MADELINE: A man was once locked in and forgotten. His skeleton was found many years later, still chained to the wall. No one could hear the cries—the walls are so thick.

LUCY: Edwin and I are betrothed. Do I have to explain how civilised people behave?

MADELINE: He said that I was a wild thing.

LUCY: I don't wish to hurt you, Madeline, any more than you wish to hurt me. But I intend to remove Edwin from temptation as soon as possible. Do you understand?

MADELINE: Oh, yes. I cannot marry Edwin while you are alive.

LUCY. Plainer terms than I would have used, but . . .

MADELINE: That is why I must kill you.

LUCY: Why . . .

MADELINE: Don't be frightened. It is quite easy to die when you have to. My father discovered that. You are not frightened are you?

LUCY: I should like to spank you. Now where are the stairs?

MADELINE: I should not like you to be frightened. My bird was frightened.

LUCY: I am waiting for you to show me the way.

MADELINE: The cells are over yonder.

LUCY: We are not going to the cells.

MADELINE: But we must, so that I can lock you in. The chains are there ready. You will let me chain you to the wall, won't you? Come now. If you won't come with me, I shall have to pull you. I am very strong.

LUCY: I am not amused by these Hallowe'en tricks. Which of these passages leads to the stairs? If you will not show me, I shall look for myself.

MADELINE: If you struggle, I may hurt you, and I do not want to hurt you because we are like sisters. You said that we were to be like sisters.

LUCY *hurries towards an exit.*

MADELINE: That is the burial chamber.

LUCY *recoils with a cry.*

MADELINE: You *are* frightened.

LUCY: Please. Please.

MADELINE: Dear Lucy.

LUCY: Very well, you did frighten me. I admit it. Are you satisfied? Now will you take me from this dreadful place?

MADELINE: No.

LUCY: You—you don't really mean to murder me?

MADELINE: Yes.

LUCY: You—you can't. You can't.

MADELINE: Would you rather I squeezed your throat?

LUCY: You can't.

MADELINE: You are so far away. You must come closer if I am to put my hands around your neck.

LUCY: You are Madeline ...

MADELINE: Or I must come closer to you.

LUCY: Have you forgotten who I am? We shared everything—my room, my clothes. You would be mad to . . .

MADELINE: They say my grandfather was mad . . . Are you about to faint, Lucy?

LUCY: No. No, I mustn't.

MADELINE: If you faint, I shall carry you. In my arms. Why do you dart about so? If you run away, you will only be lost. The candle is here. You would be fumbling in the dark without it.

LUCY (*whispering*): The candle.

MADELINE: You are not used to it as I am.

Lucy edges towards the candle.

LUCY: What good would my death do you?

MADELINE: I shall marry Edwin.

LUCY: Would he marry a murderer?

MADELINE: I shall marry Edwin.

LUCY: You will be caught and hanged.

MADELINE: I shall marry Edwin.

LUCY: Locked in prison?

MADELINE: Marry Edwin.

LUCY: You would not even see him.

MADELINE: Marry.

LUCY: You would destroy the very thing you want.

By now she has reached the candle, and picks it up. She backs towards an opening, glancing behind her to make sure of the way.

MADELINE: That is the passage under the lake. Smell the stale water. There is a pit at the end. Once prisoners were thrown into it. They fell on to spikes at the bottom. I would not like you to stumble into the pit.

Lucy *changes her direction.*

Madeline: That is the way to my cell.

Lucy *makes for another opening.*

Madeline: I told you that was the burial chamber.

Lucy *stands irresolutely in the centre of the vault.*

Madeline: This is the way to the stairs. Here, where I am standing.

Lucy: I do not want to struggle against you, Madeline.

Madeline: I shall marry Edwin.

Lucy: Not while I live.

She makes a sudden movement towards the exit. Madeline *catches her arm.*

Madeline: I told you that I was very strong.

Slowly she draws Lucy *towards the centre of the vault.*

Lucy: No.

Madeline: You will not return to Edwin, Lucy. It is time for you to die.

Lucy: No.

She pushes against Madeline *with both hands.* Madeline *blows the candle out.* Lucy *drops it.*

Madeline: Now I am holding your arms. I can feel your shoulders. And your neck. Now?

Lucy *screams.* Madeline *laughs.*

Edwin (*off*): Lucy. Lucy.

He and Roderick *rush into the vault, carrying candles.*

In the renewed light, Lucy *can be seen lying on the floor.* Madeline *stands at some distance from her. She looks mildly surprised at the hurried entrance.* EDWIN *kneels by the side of* LUCY.

EDWIN: Lucy!

RODERICK: What have you done?

EDWIN: Lucy . . .

MADELINE: She dropped the candle. The light went out.

She picks up the candle, and hands it to RODERICK. *He relights it.*

EDWIN: Was that all?

MADELINE: The darkness was too black for her.

LUCY *stirs and moans.*

RODERICK: I heard.

MADELINE: She will go now, Roderick.

LUCY: No, no . . .

EDWIN: There, there. You are quite safe.

LUCY: Where . . .

EDWIN: I am with you, my dear.

LUCY: Edwin? I prayed . . .

EDWIN: You fainted. Who can wonder in this place? You shouldn't have ventured down here.

LUCY: She . . . She . . .

EDWIN: Who?

LUCY: Her hands . . . My neck . . .

EDWIN: There are no marks. You have been frightened, that is all. Poor Lucy.

LUCY (*struggling to her feet*): Don't let her come near.

MADELINE: I am sorry. I was playing.

LUCY: Take me away from here, Edwin. From this house. Take me away.

EDWIN: But, my dear . . .

LUCY: Take me away. Take me away. (*She breaks down into sobs.*)

EDWIN: Very well.

LUCY: Take me away.

EDWIN: There there.

LUCY: Take me away. Take me away. Take me away.

They go out, EDWIN *taking one candle from* RODERICK *as he passes.*

RODERICK: Thank you, Madeline.

ACT TWO

Scene Seven

USHER

RODERICK *and* MADELINE *stand listening.*

RODERICK: Hoofbeats clattering across the broken flags. Thudding over the bridge. Then fading. Fading along the old road. Gone.

Pause. MADELINE *sits.*

RODERICK: Now we are left as we were. You and I alone. That is as it must be—you and I alone. Where else can we find solace except in each other's company? . . . This was an empty victory for me, Madeline. I would so much rather . . .

Pause.

RODERICK: Shall I read to you, my dear? As I used to. One of your favourite romances, eh? Knights, dragons, and all the rest of it.

Pause.

MADELINE: He will come back.

RODERICK: Or play for you. I shall ask Finn to bring my lute.

MADELINE: I held him with my eyes. I closed his mouth with mine.

RODERICK: We have each other. A ghost maybe of what we would desire, but all that we can trust in.

MADELINE: I could pull him, even to my grave.

RODERICK: Remember, we are of the House of Usher.

MADELINE: You are a coward, Roderick. You quiver like a mouse.

RODERICK: Let's not quarrel, my dear. We must help each other.

MADELINE: How they must laugh at your grovelling. Them. The Usher dead. The bogies that frightened you in the nursery. Empty sockets staring, dried fingers clawing, evil voices rustling. For us. One day they will have us.

RODERICK: Turnip lanterns. Reality is so much more hideous.

MADELINE: Be like me and spit at Them. I can live until I am crushed. Even a beetle does that much. I shall defy Them. I am a woman. It is part of a woman's life to marry, and have children.

RODERICK: Not you, Madeline.

MADELINE: I shall marry, and have children.

RODERICK: You must try to be happy here. Is your room too gloomy? We'll change it—gilded mirrors to catch the light, bright paints to cheer the walls, fresh hangings with new pictures—flowers, birds, butterflies. I'll send away for them now. Yes, now. You like prettty toys, don't you? You shall have them—trinkets, musical boxes, dolls. I want you to be happy.

MADELINE: You will send for anything to make me happy?

RODERICK: Anything.

MADELINE: Then send for Edwin.

Pause.

MADELINE: Or do not send for him. But he will come. What will you do when Edwin returns, Roderick? What will you do when he comes back for me?

RODERICK: I shall be prepared.

MADELINE: How?

RODERICK: That is my secret.

MADELINE: Why stare at your hands, Roderick?

RODERICK: I want to remember them—without blood on them.

CURTAIN

ACT THREE

Scene One

LUCY'S HOUSE

LUCY and EDWIN enter. She is wearing her cloak. He takes it from her. There is a strained silence between them. LUCY looks around the room.

LUCY: Home.

She turns to EDWIN. *He looks away awkwardly, and lays the cloak on the seat.*

LUCY: No apology.

EDWIN: You are tired. You'll be refreshed in the morning.

LUCY: After another night of bad dreams?

EDWIN: It was a wearing journey. Bogs, mountains, and blasted heaths. Rattling over roads that shake all reasonable notions out of your head. We should never have undertaken it in such haste.

LUCY: You believe we could have slept in that house?

EDWIN: We were guests—even though we hardly behaved as such.

LUCY: Our hosts were not exactly perfect.

EDWIN: I thought you had a sense of proportion.

LUCY: And so the quarrel goes on.

EDWIN: I am not . . .

LUCY: Mile after dreary mile.

EDWIN: I do not intend . . .

LUCY: Spurts of contradiction marking the way like signposts.

EDWIN: To quarrel.

LUCY: We are quarrelling now.

EDWIN: I haven't blamed you. It was an unfortunate accident.

LUCY: You still do not believe that she meant to murder me.

EDWIN: It was a prank—ill-judged, in bad taste, but no more.

LUCY: There is a devil in her.

EDWIN: She has always been treated as a child: can you wonder that sometimes she behaves childishly?

LUCY: She is no more a child than I am. She is a grown woman with the habits of a jackdaw, and the scruples of a shark. You see her as a dark enchantment, an elfin creature in a fairy castle. She is not. She is not. What she is, I cannot say and keep your respect. Any blame I put to her is evidence of my ill nature. But she has dazzled you. Infatuated . . . You could contradict me. Even if you lied, you could deny it. You love her. No, not love, love's counterfeit, an ugly word. Ugly as my passion now. But there cannot be room in your heart for both of us. If we are to share our lives, you must blot her from your mind; and if your desire burns too hot for that, then I release you from your engagement now.

EDWIN (*furious*): Thank you. I accept.

Pause.

LUCY (*quietly*): It was an unfortunate journey that we took, Edwin. I could not tell that the ways would fork.

EDWIN (*unhappily*): I behaved like a boor. I'm sorry.

LUCY: I too.

EDWIN: I spoke too hastily. I should like to take back my words.

LUCY: What has been said cannot be unsaid. By either of us.

EDWIN: I will still marry you, Lucy, if you wish.

LUCY: Do you mean that we are to be as we were? Or will there be an empty shell in church beside me? There should be more to a husband than a suit of clothes and a name . . . I lost you at Usher, my dear. Neither of us should have gone to Usher. There is a strong magic about the place. It changed us. Both of us . . . I can only hope that one day the spell may wear thin, and that . . . But you are free now, Edwin. Quite free.

He kisses her, tenderly, but remotely on the cheek.

EDWIN: Bless you, Lucy.

LUCY: Now leave me. Quickly before you think I am trying to soften you with tears.

EDWIN: Goodbye.

LUCY: Where will you go now?

Pause.

LUCY: Of course. Goodbye.

EDWIN *goes*.

LUCY *watches him go, then suddenly changes her mind. She calls after him.*

LUCY: Edwin.

She snatches up the cloak, and hurries to the door.

LUCY: Edwin. Edwin. Edwin.

She stops, realising what a hopeless situation it is.

LUCY (*in a despairing whisper*): Edwin.

ACT THREE

Scene Two

USHER

MADELINE (*in darkness, taking over from* LUCY'*s voice*): Edwin. Edwin.

MADELINE *is by the window, through which red sunset streams.*

MADELINE: Wind rising. Crimson waves curling over the tarn. Tattered clouds flying into the sun.

She turns and faces the centre of the room.

MADELINE: Usher dead. Can you hear me, Usher dead? Bring him to me. Bring him. Bring him.

She realises that EDWIN has entered silently and stands watching her.

MADELINE: What are you? Flesh and blood, or a spirit like them?

Pause.

MADELINE: Edwin?

EDWIN: Madeline.

MADELINE: Edwin!

She runs to him. He hurries to her. They kiss.

MADELINE: You came to me. You came.

EDWIN: I came.

MADELINE: You'll never leave me again.

EDWIN: Never.

MADELINE: Together for eternity. Swear it.

RODERICK: Eternity is a very long time.

He walks forward into the light. MADELINE *and* EDWIN *part.*

RODERICK: I am always intruding. However, I should remind you that voices resound through the house . . . A sudden re-appearance, Edwin. I understood you had returned to Town. I must reprove Finn. You were not announced. A pity. Under the circumstances this meeting appears furtive.

EDWIN: From today everything shall be as open as the sky. I am free to marry Madeline.

RODERICK: Your obligation to Lucy?

EDWIN: Ended with her consent. Is the situation clear to you now?

RODERICK: Every moth believes it can dance in a flame and not be burned. Oh, why did you come to this place? Why did you not leave sooner? Why did you return?

EDWIN: To ask your blessing. Dear fellow, wish us joy.

RODERICK: Of hell-fire?

EDWIN: Don't be cynical. I am to marry your sister.

RODERICK: You are mistaken, Edwin. I have not given consent.

EDWIN: You?

RODERICK: I cannot allow the poison to spread. Until now, the evil has been confined to this house. It must not be loosed. You reason like a child. Her face pleases you, so you must be married. But what comes after? Do you *want* to people the world with monsters?

EDWIN: I shall marry Madeline. No argument can alter that decision.

RODERICK: Then I shall not use—argument.

EDWIN: If we come to a test, you'll find my strength equal to yours. Your croaking gets monotonous, dear fellow. You can read the future no better than I can.

RODERICK: I can look into the past: the future is reflected there. I see my father's body swinging in front of that window. I see his grandfather in a frenzy, hacking his son to pieces—his grandfather spitted on a stake at the crossroads—his sister drowned in the tarn, the villagers jeering "witch". And what has been, will be. Look at this house, twisted as the minds that created it. Its decay is reflected in Madeline's eyes.

EDWIN: In Madeline's eyes I see love.

RODERICK: Nothing more? You cannot see ... No. The case is closed. I forbid the marriage. That is all.

MADELINE: Then we must defy you.

RODERICK: An elopement, you mean? You can be brought back, my dear. You know that. And you can be secured—if necessary in a dungeon.

EDWIN: Damn you!

RODERICK *cringes, his hands over his ears.*

EDWIN: You are not Madeline's keeper. Understand? You are not her keeper.

RODERICK: You pick your words precisely. I am her keeper.

EDWIN: She is her own mistress.

RODERICK: She will never be that.

EDWIN: Not by your consent.

RODERICK: Never. With my consent, or without it, God help her. Can't you see, man?

EDWIN: What?

RODERICK: That she is ... She is ...

EDWIN: She is—what?

RODERICK: Look at her. Only look with unbiased eyes. Look.

MADELINE: My brother is trying to warn you that I am already mad. But you do not need to be told, do you, Edwin? You know already. You have seen me tear my hair, and foam at the mouth. You have heard me howl at the moon. Or perhaps you didn't know. Then you must tell him, Roderick. Tell him that I have to be locked in my room. Tell him that I have to be tied to my bed. Tell him that I am at the mercy of a brother who believes I am mad.

RODERICK: Cunning. Cunning.

EDWIN: I am sorry for you, Roderick. You are crazed with your own fear.

RODERICK: Has it come?

EDWIN: And you will reduce Madeline to the same wretched condition unless . . .

RODERICK: Am I not responsible for my actions? Do I believe the impossible? I am Master of Usher, not the Caliph of Bagdad. What do I believe that is impossible? . . . If there were only a grain of doubt in your mind, could you risk the blight on your children—and your children's children? My forbears took the risk. There has been tragedy in every generation. We are on the threshold of a greater tragedy now. If there were only a seed . . .

EDWIN: There is not even a seed.

RODERICK: Then I must plant it.

ACT THREE

Scene Four

USHER

The DOCTOR *has joined the group.*

DOCTOR: You sent for me, sir.

EDWIN: Your minions appear too conveniently, Roderick.

RODERICK: Doctor . . .

EDWIN: Doctor?

DOCTOR: You must pardon my disarray, sir. I was caught

in my shirtsleeves. Yes—yes. Sitting down to dinner. But your man said "hurry", and I know what that means.

RODERICK: What does it mean, Doctor?

DOCTOR: Hurry? (*He glances uneasily at* MADELINE.) Why, it—er—it means hurry. Yes—yes. I dropped my spoon, grabbed my bag, and was on my way in less time that it takes to wipe the grease off my chin.

EDWIN: When could I have seen you before—Doctor?

DOCTOR: Here and there, sir. Yes—yes. Here and there. I've travelled in my time.

RODERICK: The gentleman has an interest in your patient. Will you explain the case to him.

DOCTOR: I couldn't do that, sir. No—no. A matter of honour. You understand, sir.

RODERICK: I understand that you will never receive another fee in these parts if you do not.

DOCTOR: Well, if you put it like that, sir . . . There are cases of universal importance that might be discussed. Yes—yes. With the consent of the patient.

RODERICK: Or without.

DOCTOR: But—not with the young lady present, sir.

RODERICK: You hamper the doctor, Madeline. Will you leave us?

MADELINE: No.

RODERICK: Then, doctor, you must endure my sister's presence. What is the sickness called?

DOCTOR: You'll understand this is only one man's opinion, sir. I could be wrong.

RODERICK: Could you?

DOCTOR: I'm sorry, miss. Yes—yes. The young lady's disorder is of a nervous description.

RODERICK: You used a different term to me.

DOCTOR: Dementia Praecox.

RODERICK: In English.

DOCTOR: Progressive insanity.

EDWIN: Liar!

RODERICK: You must not browbeat a witness.

EDWIN: How much were you paid to spread this malice?

DOCTOR: Bribed, do you mean, sir?

EDWIN: You'd tell any tale if you were paid enough, wouldn't you?

DOCTOR: I'm paid my fee, sir. That's all. Yes—yes. And a poor enough living I make. This is rough country, sir.

RODERICK: There is no loophole, Edwin.

EDWIN: When did you leave the city, Doctor?

DOCTOR: I had an urge to wander, sir.

EDWIN: The urge to hide?

DOCTOR: Why should I want to hide?

EDWIN: Why indeed? There's rich harvest in the city. Why leave those pickings to dine on thin broth?

RODERICK: You have bullied him long enough, Edwin.

DOCTOR: I'm a simple physician, sir. Yes—yes. Working in a far country for suffering humanity.

EDWIN: What's your name?

DOCTOR: My name?

EDWIN: The man I heard of was called Burke. But what's a name when you change it oftner than your shirt. He had such a face as yours—sore-rimmed eyes, spirit-flushed nose.

RODERICK: Don't vent your spleen on the doctor, Edwin. He has served me in his fashion.

EDWIN: To keep Madeline in subjection?

DOCTOR: But I have proof—begging your pardon, miss—wild talk, sleep-walking, unnatural doings.

EDWIN: Shall I tell you what I know of Doctor Burke?

DOCTOR: It can hardly concern me, sir.

EDWIN: His story was all over the town. He disappeared suddenly a few months ago. Before that he had specialised in relieving the distress of—over-generous ladies. As the birth-rate went down, his fees went up. But if a secret is worth keeping, it is worth paying to keep. His patients found themselves suffering from consumption of the pocket. Isn't that so, Doctor?

DOCTOR: I wouldn't know, sir.

EDWIN: Until one husband, loving his wife enough to forgive, and resenting the hush-money paid from his own coffers, announced his intention of running a rapier through the doctor's carcase. The quack took flight. But the hunt is not over. If that husband could find the criminal, he would have his revenge yet. It would take two days for the news to reach the town—less, perhaps, to bring retribution here. What is your name, Doctor? Unless your conscience is quite clear, you have four days—less if you wish to cover your trail. I advise you to start now. Now.

Pause. The DOCTOR *gets up, and walks slowly to the door.*

DOCTOR: God help me . . . I thought myself safe. Who would come raking up the past among old stones? But I cannot escape my own shadow. I'll take my leave of your gentlemen—madam. I must be getting back to my dinner. The broth must be cold by now. You'll not see me again, sir . . . But I can tell you this—the time's fast coming when you would wish to.

He hurries out.

RODERICK: Doctor!

MADELINE: Poor man.

EDWIN: There goes the proof that was to shake my faith.

RODERICK: Blind. Blind.

MADELINE: He loves me, Roderick.

EDWIN: How much further will you go to dishonour Madeline?

RODERICK: I want to keep her from dishonour.

MADELINE: I shall wear a white bridal gown.

EDWIN: Your obsession and your misfortune are the same—a too legible pedigree. Destroy that—not Madeline's happiness.

RODERICK: Marriage—happiness?

MADELINE: After the wedding we shall keep a house in Town.

RODERICK: Joy to become a breeder of madmen?

EDWIN: Even the Usher fold must have been blessed by the occasional white sheep. Which Usher beauty handed down her bloom to Madeline?

RODERICK: Up there she hangs—that portrait there. Do you see? She burned in this life, if not in the next. At the stake.

EDWIN: You cannot resign from the human race. Behind these walls you are still one of us.

The house rumbles.

EDWIN: Break, then. Break. And let daylight in.

RODERICK: You have mistaken the time. You mean surrender to the darkness.

MADELINE: And I must have a cradle. For the baby when he comes.

EDWIN puts his arm around her. RODERICK turns away, hand over mouth, choking back nausea.

ACT THREE

Scene Five

USHER

The barest glimmer of light comes from the window. RODERICK is kneeling alone. FINN enters with a candle. RODERICK looks up, then stands up. FINN hands the candle to him.

RODERICK: It has been done?

FINN mimes breaking a stick.

RODERICK: And then?

FINN mimes someone walking upstairs, hand on banisters. The banisters wobble, and climber falls outwards. He mimes an onlooker, peering and pointing below. He mimes a man dead with a broken neck.

RODERICK: You must make sure that my sister does not accompany him up the stairs.

FINN nods and withdraws.

RODERICK: Now—a murderer. One step more. Nearer and nearer to the brink.

The house rumbles. Roderick looks upwards.

RODERICK: Hurl your damned thunderbolt. Hurl it, and we'll all go to Hell.

He runs out.

ACT THREE

Scene Six

A Corridor

Finn enters, looks behind him, then slips into darkness. Edwin enters with Madeline. They each carry a candle. They pause.

EDWIN: Goodnight, my sweet. Our ways part here.

MADELINE: Must they?

EDWIN: Until you are Mrs. Allen. Goodnight.

He turns towards the stairs.

MADELINE: Where are you going?

EDWIN: Aloft. Where else? To bed.

MADELINE: You must be mistaken.

EDWIN: My old room developed draughts, damp, or some such ailment.

MADELINE: But no-one ever goes up there. Ever.

EDWIN: I am a stranger. I'm not acquainted with all the Usher legends.

MADELINE: I have always been told that—that . . .

EDWIN: These stairs were pointed out to me.

MADELINE: Roderick wants to—to . . . If an accident happened . . .

EDWIN: What could happen? There are no ghosts up there.

MADELINE: There are ghosts everywhere, of one sort and another.

EDWIN: I shan't let myself be swallowed alive.

MADELINE: I shall come with you.

EDWIN: Then Roderick *would* have cause for suspicion.

MADELINE: I shall see you safely to your room. If anything happens to you, it must also happen to me.

EDWIN: Your strange, romantic notions ...

MADELINE: Don't laugh. Please.

EDWIN: But I insist that you come no further than the door of my room. I can be strict when I choose.

MADELINE *takes his arm. Before they have advanced more than a few steps towards the stairs,* FINN *emerges from his hiding place, and holds* MADELINE *back.*

EDWIN: But soft, we are observed. Your brother is more suspicious than I thought. We must humour him, though. I'll continue my journey alone.

MADELINE: No. Finn shall light your way.

FINN *does not move.*

EDWIN: I am capable of holding my own candlestick.

MADELINE: Finn shall do it.

EDWIN: Will you be so good as to light me to my room?

He hands his candle to FINN, *who still does not move.*

EDWIN: Do you believe in bogeymen, too? Your master can hardly expect me to sleep comfortably in a place his own servants shy at.

MADELINE: Unless you climb those stairs in front of Mr. Edwin, he shall spend the night in my room. Do you understand? Now, go.

FINN *releases her, and looks from her to* EDWIN.

MADELINE: Up. Up. Is there something you would rather not face at the top of the stairs?

FINN *takes a few steps towards the stairs, then stops.*

MADELINE: Up, Finn. Up.

FINN *goes nearer to the stairs, then turns to face* MADELINE *and* EDWIN.

MADELINE: You see?

EDWIN: What is wrong with those stairs?

MADELINE: An accident could happen to anyone up there. The wood is pocked with fungus, and smells of mould. It crumbles. If you were to fall, it would be—just an accident. But, afterwards you would not be able to marry me.

EDWIN: Climb, man. Climb.

FINN *does not move.*

EDWIN: If you won't go in front, at least you shall come with me.

He tries to lead FINN *towards the stairs.* FINN *pushes him away, thrusts the candle into his hand, and runs from the gallery.*

EDWIN: So there is a trap.

MADELINE: There are traps everywhere. The house is against you. You are not safe.

EDWIN: A house cannot hurt me.

MADELINE: Stones can fall, beams can break.

EDWIN: They can when a man arranges it. You think your brother has other diversions for me?

MADELINE: Not Roderick. Them.

EDWIN: Them?

MADELINE: The Usher dead.

EDWIN: You don't believe such moonshine.

MADELINE: No. No, of course not. I—I laugh at them. They lie in their tomb deep down below us. No-one ever leaves their tomb, do they? An absurd notion. Roderick laughs at it, too. Though sometimes, They make him do strange things like . . . We—he—cannot help himself. They are very powerful. That is—They would be if anyone believed in Them. We made silly jokes about Them when we were children. About the way They see into every corner of the house, the way their fingers grow like reeds through their coffin lids. Foolishness. Children's tales. There are no Usher dead. They are dead. Dead. That is why we must leave. Leave quickly. Or we shall never escape them. I have always laughed at Them. I have laughed at Them for not being there. They do not like to be laughed at. They hate you for wanting to marry me. They say I must not marry. But why should we take notice of Them? They don't exist. They have never . . . Never. They say that I must never . . . Never. So we must . . . We must . . . Never. Ever. Run. Run. Run now. Or never. Ever. Ever.

EDWIN: Madeline!

MADELINE: Run. Run away.

EDWIN: You're . . .

MADELINE: Away.

EDWIN: This is hysteria.

MADELINE: Way. Way. Way.

EDWIN (*shaking her*): Listen to me.

MADELINE: Ay. Ay. Ay.

EDWIN *smacks her face. She gives a little cry.*

MADELINE: Who? . . . You.

EDWIN: I'm sorry, my darling. You must keep your self-control until we are out of this pest-hole.

MADELINE: Yes.

EDWIN: We shall leave at once. Take no more than you need. I shall take care of the rest.

MADELINE: Yes.

EDWIN: Quickly.

MADELINE: Yes.

EDWIN: Finn will have had time to report to his master.

MADELINE: Yes.

ACT THREE

Scene Seven

USHER

RODERICK *kneels by the seat. His head is hidden in his arms.*

MADELINE *enters, walking like a somnambulist. She clutches a knife in her hand.* RODERICK *raises his head, but does not turn to her.*

RODERICK: I know why you have come. Cold reason lures us into madder action than ever madness could. But the attempt was abortive, thank God. He'll live to take you away. (*He stands, turns, and sees the knife.*) You have brought that knife for me?

She nods.

RODERICK: Is it a sharp knife?

She nods.

RODERICK: Do you hate me so much.

She takes a step towards him. He flinches.

RODERICK: Once you loved me.

She shakes her head.

RODERICK: Years ago. We were children then. You would come to me for protection. Remember? When father beat you because you were too slow answering—or too fast.

When he locked you in the turret with only bread and water. You would come to me. In those days our only happiness was found with each other. The years passed like a long freezing night. Remember? Wretched, happy time. Until you withdrew into your other strange world . . . Come to me now.

She shakes her head, and hugs the knife protectively.

RODERICK: You may keep your knife. I don't want to take anything from you.

She shakes her head.

RODERICK: Come, Madeline . . . Come.

Slowly she goes to him. He sits her down, and puts his arms around her.

RODERICK: You're shivering. (*He puts his hand over hers.*) Your hands are cold as snow. No, I don't want your knife. You hold it. Edwin imagines that he loves you. But will he care for you when you slip into that other world? Or will he deliver you to worse gaolers than I? The madhouse is a savage place. I have never wished to do anything but protect you. The other Madeline—she up there—had no protection. She died in the fire. A witch. She would sleep as though dead, and ignorant clods swore that she sent her soul to torment them. But that poor creature was guilty of nothing worse than a trance. A cataleptic trance. The same catalepsy that plagues you.

MADELINE *gets up suddenly.*

RODERICK: It does, my dear.

MADELINE: No.

RODERICK: Remember the days that vanish from the calendar?

MADELINE: I—I . . .

RODERICK: The clock that lies about the time.

MADELINE: I—I must leave.

RODERICK: You must stay with me.

MADELINE: Leave. Leave quickly.

RODERICK: If you ever loved me.

MADELINE: I—I hate you.

RODERICK: Hate?

MADELINE: Hate. Hate. Hate.

RODERICK: If you hate me so much, why didn't you kill me?

MADELINE: Kill—you?

RODERICK: Why not kill me now?

MADELINE: Kill.

RODERICK: You have the knife in your hand. A sharp knife, isn't it? One blow here, and the thing you hate would be dead.

MADELINE: Yes.

RODERICK: Well? . . . You hate me, remember. You never loved me.

She approaches him with the knife. She raises the knife. She wimpers, turns away, and drops it.

RODERICK: My dear . . .

MADELINE: Listen.

RODERICK: To what.

MADELINE: Them.

RODERICK: Them?

MADELINE: They are calling.

RODERICK: Calling to you?

MADELINE: Yes. Come to us, they call.

RODERICK: Of course.

MADELINE: We are waiting, they call.

RODERICK: Waiting for you?

MADELINE: Waiting.

RODERICK: We are waiting, they say.

MADELINE: Yes.

RODERICK: Here in the dark.

MADELINE: Yes.

RODERICK: We are waiting in the dark. For you. You. Here.

Gently he caresses her, crooning the words. She stands absolutely still, staring ahead of her.

RODERICK: Here in the dark. The dark is waiting. Waiting for you. Think of us, Madeline. Us. The dead. Think of the dead, Madeline. The dead. We are at peace. Peace. Death brings peace, Madeline. Death and peace. Sleep and peace. Sleep. Death and sleep. In the dark. The dark. Death and the dark. Think of the dark, Madeline. And death. Dark death. Peaceful death. In the dark. You will sleep in the dark. At peace in the dark. Dead in the dark. Asleep. At peace. Sleep at peace. Peace. Sleep. Sleep. Cold. You are cold, Madeline. Cold as death. Cold as sleep. Sleep. Sleep . . .

He pauses. Silence. He waves his hand in front of MADELINE's *eyes. She does not blink. He closes her eyes.*

RODERICK: Lie still. Still.

He supports her body on to the ground.

RODERICK: He will not take you away now.

FINN *enters with* MADELINE's *cloak.* RODERICK *stands.* FINN *holds out the cloak.* RODERICK *takes it from him.*

RODERICK: She will hardly need it now. Instead you had better prepare her coffin.

FINN *stares at the body.*

RODERICK: I said her coffin. It has been standing long enough in readiness.

FINN *points to the body.*

RODERICK: Yes. She is dead. It was her heart, you understand. Her heart. She had better lie in her coffin. Appearances. Appearances. Let me know when it is ready.

FINN *goes.*

RODERICK *kneels by* MADELINE. *He crosses her hands on her breast. Then he spreads the cloak over her, leaving only her face exposed.*

RODERICK: Don't wake too soon, Madeline. Forgive me for what I must do to you. But it is for your own sake. And it will not be for long. I shall release you as soon as he has gone. If you should wake, my dear . . . If you should wake . . . Don't be afraid of the dark. There are worse things to fear than the dark.

He hears someone coming. He kneels, and assumes an attitude of prayer.

EDWIN *bursts in.*

EDWIN: What damned new folly is this?

RODERICK: Sssh!

EDWIN: What have you done to her?

RODERICK: Don't touch her. She is at peace.

EDWIN: She can't . . .

RODERICK: Her heart could not stand the strain.

EDWIN: I don't believe you. I won't believe you.

RODERICK: I tried to warn you. She died in my arms.

EDWIN: Madeline. Madeline.

RODERICK: You didn't remark any strangeness in her behaviour? I recognised the signs. I realised at once that she was in danger. Desperately. Only the doctor could have helped. And I doubt if he could have reached her in time.

EDWIN: She's alive.

RODERICK: The end came suddenly.

EDWIN: Alive, I tell you.

RODERICK: You cannot lend even your vigour to a corpse.

EDWIN: There's colour in her cheeks.

RODERICK: A symptom of her malady. A pity you thrust the doctor away so brutally. He might have convinced you.

EDWIN: She's warm. Feel. (*He puts his hand to her cheek, but is taken aback by what he feels.*) Feel.

RODERICK: Cold already? Her heart has stopped, her blood congealing. (*He pulls back the cloak.*) Take her pulse.

EDWIN *feels her pulse, and looks blankly at* RODERICK.

RODERICK: Is there a flutter—ever so feeble?

EDWIN *shakes his head.*

RODERICK: Wait. Here is a knife. The blade is as polished as a mirror. Hold it over her mouth—so.

He holds the blade over MADELINE's *mouth, then shows the blade to* EDWIN.

RODERICK: Has it clouded? Does she breathe?

EDWIN: I held her to me only a minute ago.

RODERICK: You will never hold her in your arms again.

EDWIN: You would rather have seen her dead than married to me.

RODERICK: My dear Edwin, you were her angel of destruction. Your haste destroyed her.

EDWIN: I loved her.

RODERICK: You are not the first man to kill what he loved. Nor will you be the last.

EDWIN: What am I to do now?

RODERICK: You will resume your natural life.

EDWIN: I can't—I can't leave her.

RODERICK: You cannot linger in the tomb with her. Ride back to Town, and forget her. It will not be too difficult—a ball or so, a couple of cock-fights, another pretty face, and the memory will fade.

EDWIN: She is to be buried?

RODERICK: What else?

EDWIN: She looks so ... so ...

RODERICK: Alive? Young? Fresh? The grave isn't reserved for the old and ugly. It's a democratic place. We all come to it.

EDWIN: I want to stay with her. Until the end.

RODERICK: Until the funeral is over? Could you bear to see the coffin lid closed over her?

EDWIN: Until I do, I shall never believe that she will not come back.

RODERICK: It is an answer I expected. You shall be there when she is committed to the tomb.

EDWIN: I would have died for her, cheerfully. She was to have been my wife.

RODERICK: No, dear fellow. This was her destiny. Fate was the enemy. Your defeat was certain. Accept it. Accept it.

EDWIN: I won't.

RODERICK: What is there to hope for? I told you—hope is a delusion. There is no hope in hell's mouth.

Finn enters.

RODERICK: The coffin is ready.

ACT THREE

Scene Eight

THE VAULT

MADELINE lies in her coffin. Her face is lit by two candles which burn at the head of the coffin. EDWIN kneels at one side of the coffin. FINN kneels at the other. RODERICK kneels at the foot of the coffin. The three men stand.

RODERICK dismisses FINN with an inclination of the head.

FINN goes into the burial chamber.

EDWIN (*turning towards the burial chamber*): It's too soon, Give me a little longer with her. Too soon. (*Covers his face.*)

RODERICK goes to him, and puts a hand on his shoulder.

MADELINE *moans.*

RODERICK looks sharply behind him.

MADELINE raises an arm as though pushing something away. Then the arm is relaxed, and hangs over the edge of the coffin. RODERICK backs silently from EDWIN, and turns to MADELINE. He re-crosses her hands.

RODERICK: The lid must be closed. It would be easier for you, if you did not turn until I had finished.

He places the lid on the coffin. There is a slight thud as it falls into position.

EDWIN: One last glimpse.

RODERICK shakes his head, and fastens down the lid.

EDWIN: My life is locked there, too.

He throws himself at the coffin, hugging it. Suddenly he looks up.

EDWIN: A sigh. I heard a sigh . . . Did I hear a sigh?

RODERICK *shakes his head pityingly.*

FINN *returns.*

EDWIN: Must she?

RODERICK *and* FINN *carry the coffin out.* EDWIN *takes a step or two after them, then sobbing overcomes him. He sinks to his knees with his hands clasped.* RODERICK *returns with* FINN.

RODERICK: Courage, my dear fellow.

EDWIN: I miss your stoic upbringing. Tragedy comes raw to me. Only yesterday . . .

RODERICK: You must think of the days to come. You'll find a weight lift once you are clear of these walls. Finn shall see you on your way.

EDWIN: Tonight? An abrupt dismissal.

RODERICK: No. No, of course not tonight. But in a few hours it will be daylight. Surely you don't wish to linger.

EDWIN: I only wish to mourn her. At least grant me time for that. I—I cannot face the road. She calls to me.

RODERICK: No doubt. She—she calls to both of us.

He hands a candle to FINN, *who takes it to the exit.* FINN *stops and looks back at* EDWIN. EDWIN *follows him.* RODERICK *starts for the entrance, but is jerked back. He stares towards the burial chamber.*

RODERICK: No, Madeline. Don't scream. It rings in my ears. I beg of you. Don't scream. Don't scream. Don't scream. Don't scream!

ACT THREE

Scene Nine

USHER

RODERICK *sits holding a closed book.*

RODERICK (*suddenly he listens*): Don't, Madeline. Don't!

He slams the book on to the seat beside him, and jumps up. He takes a few irresolute steps towards the door.

There comes a flicker of lightning through the window.

RODERICK: It will be soon now, Madeline. I swear. We shall be alone. Then you will be free. Only be still. You are tearing your fingers. Be still.

Low rumble of thunder.

RODERICK *hears someone coming, picks up the book, and sits as though calmly reading.*

FINN *enters.*

RODERICK: Are the horses saddled? He must have no reason to turn back. Make sure of that. He must not turn back. Where is he?

FINN *makes a beckoning gesture.*

RODERICK: Be ready to ride with him. There has been too much delay. It will soon be sunset again . . . Do you hear, Finn? Hear the scratching—like rats in the wood? Scratching. Scratching.

FINN *shakes his head.*

RODERICK: Strange. I thought everyone would have heard . . . Go down to the vaults. Take as many candles as you can carry. Light them all.

FINN *hesitates.*

RODERICK: Don't question me, man. Have candles burning outside the burial chamber.

EDWIN *enters, dressed for travelling.*

EDWIN: Waiting for me? I'll not be long.

FINN *bows and withdraws.*

EDWIN: Time for farewells, Roderick. If only we could have parted with smiles.

RODERICK: I—I doubt if we shall ever see each other again.

Thunder.

EDWIN *goes to the window.*

EDWIN: At least the outlook is appropriate. The tarn rears up like an animal in rage. It's wild weather for travellers.

RODERICK: You should have set out earlier.

Lightning. EDWIN *staggers back.*

RODERICK: What happened?

EDWIN: The lightning ran like a sword under the water.

Thunder.

RODERICK: Goodbye, Edwin.

EDWIN: Goodbye?

RODERICK: You came to say goodbye. If you delay, you'll be contending with the night as well as the elements.

EDWIN: I can brave a wetting, but I don't want the horses to take fright.

Lightning, followed closely by thunder.

RODERICK: Be still!

EDWIN: You can't control the storm.

RODERICK: Not the storm. Not the storm. Judgement day has come. I must be mad now. Am I? Am I mad.

Lightning.

EDWIN: No.

RODERICK: No. Madness would be a release. But it must come. Soon. Strike me, then. Strike me.

EDWIN: Gently. Gently.

RODERICK: I am afraid . . . My ears.

EDWIN: We must drown the thunder, then. Shall I read to you?

Lightning.

RODERICK *gives a cry.*

RODERICK: She struggles. She struggles. So desperately.

EDWIN: Sit down.

He leads RODERICK *to the seat, and picks up the book.*

RODERICK *sits.*

EDWIN *opens the book.*

EDWIN: Is this your marker?

Lightning, followed almost immediately by two claps of thunder.

EDWIN (*reading*): "And Lancelot, who was mighty withal, waited no longer to hold parley, but, fearing the rising of the tempest, uplifted his mace outright, and, with blows, made quickly room in the plankings of the door for his gauntleted hand. And now pulling therewith sturdily, he is ripped and tore all asunder, that the noise of the dry and hollow-sounding wood reverberated throughout . . ."

RODERICK (*jumping to his feet*): No! It is not possible. It is not possible!

Lightning and thunder simultaneously.

EDWIN: Did that strike us? (*He runs to the window.*)

RODERICK: Was it possible?

EDWIN: I don't see anything. It could have been another part of the building.

RODERICK: Silence now. No more scratching.

The house rumbles. EDWIN *looks up.*

EDWIN: Look!

RODERICK: Where?

EDWIN: The fissure. Wider. I could thrust my hand into the crack.

RODERICK: It had to happen.

EDWIN: The house is doomed.

RODERICK: It was doomed from the moment the foundation stone was laid.

Lightning.

RODERICK: You must go. The horses are waiting.

Thunder.

EDWIN: Hurry. Hurry.

He makes for the door, but realises that RODERICK *is not following.*

EDWIN: Move, man. Move.

RODERICK: I must wait.

EDWIN: Why?

RODERICK: For—with—Madeline. I mustn't leave her.

EDWIN: If the house is safe for you, it is safe for me.

A rumble. EDWIN *deliberately picks up the book again, and opens it.*

EDWIN (*reading*): "But the good champion now entering within was amazed to perceive a dragon, which sat on guard. And Lancelot uplifted his mace, and struck upon the head of the dragon, which fell before him with a shriek so horrid and harsh . . ."

From outside comes a long drawn-out scream, followed by a crash of masonry falling.

EDWIN: Mercy!

He throws down the book and runs out.

RODERICK: No sound now. No sound.

EDWIN *returns, half-supporting, half-dragging* FINN. FINN *is bloody, and covered with fallen plaster.*

EDWIN: Half the ceiling is down. The corridor is piled with rubble.

He lays FINN *down.*

EDWIN: He was struck by a falling cornice.

FINN *stirs, and tries to raise himself.*

EDWIN: Lie still. You are hurt.

FINN *still struggles.* EDWIN *helps him up to a sitting position.*

FINN *shakes his head, and tries to mouth words.*

EDWIN: Struggles will only make you worse. What are you trying to tell me?

FINN *tries to indicate by jerking his head.*

EDWIN: Out there?

FINN *nods.*

EDWIN: The beam collapsed.

FINN *shakes his head.*

EDWIN: You saw something else.

FINN *nods.*

EDWIN: Something that put an almighty fear into you. Was it the wall?

FINN *shakes his head.*

EDWIN: Something besides falling masonry.

FINN *nods and tries to force out words.*

EDWIN: What are you trying to say?

RODERICK: He can't speak.

FINN: Ma . . .

EDWIN: He spoke then.

RODERICK: Impossible.

FINN: Ma . . . Ma . . . (*He forces himself from* EDWIN's *arms.*) Madeline!

He falls back. EDWIN *lowers him to the ground.*

EDWIN: Dead.

RODERICK: He said . . . He said . . .

EDWIN: What did he mean?

RODERICK; He saw her.

EDWIN: Nonsense.

RODERICK: As I heard her.

EDWIN: When?

RODERICK: Ever since . . . Ever . . . I heard—while you were reading. I heard her blows on the coffin lid. I heard her rending the wood. Madness must have given her the strength.

EDWIN: Fantasy.

RODERICK: She escaped. But the fall that killed Finn gave her a rougher burial.

EDWIN: I saw her dead. The dead cannot walk.

RODERICK: It was the catalepsy. We buried her alive—you and I. I risked everything on your leaving us once you believed her dead. But you insisted on seeing her placed in the mausoleum. She has lain there all this time. Alive.

EDWIN: This is delirium.

RODERICK: And—and she is still alive. Scrabbling over the stones.

EDWIN: Out there?

He turns towards the entrance, but RODERICK *holds his arm.*

RODERICK: Are you mad, too?

EDWIN: She needs help.

RODERICK: She's past all help now. A maniac.

EDWIN: Let me go!

He shakes off RODERICK. *The house rumbles. Both men stagger and fall to the floor.* MADELINE *appears in the entrance. Her hands are bloody where she has torn them, and her dress is stained. She stares around the room. The men stand.* RODERICK *and* MADELINE *look at each other for a few seconds. Then* MADELINE *screams, rushes at him, and clutches his throat in her hands. Choking, he is forced to his knees.* EDWIN *parts them.* MADELINE *staggers back, and falls by the seat. The knife with which she threatened Roderick is still lying there. She picks it up, and examines it curiously.*

MADELINE: It is a sharp knife.

The men back from her.

MADELINE: What was I saying? Oh, yes. I once had a lover. I was to marry him, and live in the city, and have children for him. But he left me. He would not marry me because my name is Usher. Ushers have a bad name. That is because they know . . They know . . . He promised never to leave me. I wish—I wish that I could have been married. But death is a remarkable experience, too. If I cannot live, at least I can die. It is quite easy to die. (*She raises the knife.*)

EDWIN: Don't!

She drives in the knife. RODERICK *catches her as she falls.*

MADELINE: Roderick?

RODERICK: My dear?

MADELINE: You mustn't be afraid.

RODERICK: I tried to prevent it. I tried.

Gently he lowers her to the ground.

EDWIN: She said I betrayed her.

RODERICK: She didn't know you. Her mind was broken.

EDWIN: I promised to stay with her—to the end.

RODERICK: Like puppets we move as we are pulled. At least she struggled. What a fright for the puppet master.

Outside more masonry falls.

EDWIN: But I shall keep my word now.

RODERICK: The wall of the vault has been breached. The tarn rushes in. Boiling, hissing, swirling, carrying everything before it.

EDWIN: It is easy to die, she said.

RODERICK: Battering at the foundations. What are you doing here, Edwin? The walls won't hold much longer. Your tears can wait.

EDWIN: Death shall not part us.

RODERICK: A romantic gesture, but quite useless. What a triumph for Usher—an innocent trapped in its very downfall. But They shall not have you, Edwin. You must marry Lucy.

EDWIN: Seed must be scattered with hope, or why sow it?

RODERICK: There can be victory even in the grave.

EDWIN: Has my tutor changed his text?

RODERICK: Yes . .. The crack is gaping wider . . . Yes, there is hope. The Usher dead toss in the water, the old bones dancing in the spray. Their power is broken.

EDWIN: Then why not save yourself?

RODERICK: I—I will. The horses are tethered by the door. We mustn't let them be hurt. No, don't look back. Remember Madeline if you must, but not her clay. The horses are screaming. Hurry. Hurry.

He pushes EDWIN towards the entrance, then stops.

RODERICK: One moment. Run ahead my dear fellow. Go. Go.

He gives EDWIN a push, which sends him on his way. He watches him go.

RODERICK: Faster. Faster. Yes. Yes. You'll reach safety. Tell Lucy that for a wedding present I sent her—a husband . . .

He smiles, goes over to MADELINE, and kneels by the body.

RODERICK: You were right, my dear. There is nothing left to fear. The disease has been cured, the poison stopped.

The house rumbles. He looks up.

RODERICK: Shake. Shake. Let it come down. The line of Usher is finished. Let its evil perish with its house. I have seen the curse ended, the fear overcome. I can watch your destruction Usher, and I am no longer afraid. Fall. Fall. I am not afraid.

A great rending and tearing as the house crashes into the tarn.

CURTAIN

CARMILLA

DAVID CAMPTON

Carmilla

*A Gothic Thriller
in Two Acts*

based on a story by
SHERIDAN LE FANU

LONDON
J. GARNET MILLER LTD

FIRST PUBLISHED BY J. GARNET MILLER LTD
IN 1973
PRINTED IN GREAT BRITAIN BY
CLARKE, DOBLE & BRENDON LIMITED, PLYMOUTH
© DAVID CAMPTON 1973

ISBN 85343 534 0

All rights reserved. An acting fee is payable on each and every performance of this play. For information regarding the fee for amateur stage performances, application should be made to the publishers: J. GARNET MILLER LTD., 1-5 Portpool Lane, London, EC1N 7SL *or to the following agents:*

Great Britain:	10 Station Road Industrial Estate, Colwall, Malvern, Worcestershire WR13 6RN *Telephone:* 01684 540154
Eire:	Fred Hanna Ltd., 28 and 29 Nassau Street, Dublin, C.3.
Australia:	Will Andrade, Box 3111, G.P.O., Sydney, N.S.W. 2001.
Kenya, Uganda and Tanganyika:	Master Play Agencies, P.O. Box 452, Nairobi, Kenya.
New Zealand:	The Play Bureau (N.Z.) Ltd., P.O. Box 3611, Wellington.
South Africa:	Darters (Pty) Ltd., P.O. Box 174, Cape Town.

Applications for all other performances should be made to: ACTAC LTD., 16 Cadogan Lane, London, S.W.1.

CAST

CAPTAIN FIELD
IVAN
LAURA
MADAME PERRODON
COLONEL SMITHSON
CARMILLA
DOCTOR SPIELSBERG

The action takes place in and around Colonel Smithson's schloss in Central Europe. The time is the early nineteenth century.

Carmilla was first presented at the Library Theatre, Scarborough on June 19th, 1972 with the following cast:

CAPTAIN FIELD	*Ray Jewers*
IVAN	*David Hayward*
LAURA	*Philippa Urquhart*
MADAME PERRODON	*Matyelock Gibbs*
COLONEL SMITHSON	*Piers Rogers*
CARMILLA	*Jennifer Piercy*
DOCTOR SPIELSBERG	*Christopher Godwin*

Directed by *Alan Ayckbourn*
Music composed by *Barrie Davenport*

PRODUCTION NOTE

This play was first staged with a permanent setting. Conventional scenery can be used, but pauses for scene changes should be kept to a minimum so that the play is allowed to flow uninterruptedly towards its climax.

In the original production a trick coffin was built which enabled the actress playing Carmilla to be hidden, while a skeleton dressed in rags fell into her place.

If it is desirable to reduce the number of sets, the castle drawing-room scenes could be played on the terrace.

ACT ONE

Scene One

A Cemetery

Darkness. In the distance a bell tolls.

CAPTAIN FIELD enters, a heavy military cloak over his uniform, and carrying a lantern.

He is an army officer in his late twenties, with resource, imagination, and—in happier circumstances—a sense of humour.

He pauses and looks about him suspiciously. He thinks he detects a movement in the shadows behind him.

FIELD (*turning*): Who's there? . . . Come out . . . Show yourself . . . I shan't ask again. I'll shoot.

IVAN materialises in the circle of light.

FIELD: You. Why are you skulking in the burial ground at his time of night?

IVAN: I might ask the same of the captain.

FIELD: You were following me . . . *Her* orders?

IVAN: I cannot answer questions about my mistress.

FIELD: You can take a message to your mistress, though. Tell her that she's a damned murderess. But you don't need to be told that. You've never been far away from that Devil's whore. How many times has she killed?

IVAN: I cannot answer questions about my mistress.

FIELD: You don't even waste your breath in denial. The girl I should have married lies cold in her grave. Is that why you have orders to follow me? Could your mistress be curious—or afraid? She has reason to be.

7

Because when I have done what must be done, I shall seek her out.

Ivan: You would be advised, Captain, not to interfere with forces you do not understand. You must fail.

Field: You mean your mistress has the powers of darkness on her side.

Ivan: I meant that my mistress leaves Paris tonight. By the time you have done—what has to be done—she will have passed beyond your feeble attempts to harm her. My mistress travels fast.

Field: "The dead travel fast". You've heard that, Ivan? But neither too fast nor too far for me. Let her fly to the poles or the tropics. I shall follow. She cannot hide, because death travels with her. You heard that bell—sure sign that your mistress passed this way. And when I do find her, I'll send her black soul screaming to Hell. Tell her that from me.

Ivan: As you wish, Captain.

With a click of the heels and a slight mocking bow he backs into the darkness.

In the distance a cock crows.

Ivan (*from the darkness*): Cockcrow, Captain. Daybreak. The first grey streaks in the sky. It is time now.

Field: Damn you!

His cloak falls open revealing a sharpened stake in his hand. He raises it like a weapon, but realises that it is useless. Ivan *has gone, and the stake was brought for a different purpose.*

Field: It is time. Forgive me, my dear. But it must be done.

He turns and strides towards the place he was making for.

After a pause there comes a scream.

ACT ONE

Scene Two

THE DRAWING-ROOM IN THE CASTLE

Sunshine and the sound of a musical box playing a waltz.

LAURA waltzes in to the tinkling tune. LAURA is about eighteen, lively and unsophisticated.

She is followed by adoring, twittering MADAME PERRODON, her middle-aged governess.

PERRODON: Oh, Mam'selle Laura.

LAURA: Dance with me, Madame Perrodon. One cannot waltz alone. One must have a partner.

PERRODON: If your papa should . . .

LAURA (*laughing*): He will say "What is Perrodon doing with my chee-ild? Court martial her at once." Dance, Madame. One-two-three. One-two-three. One-two three.

She seizes PERRODON and waltzes with her.

PERRODON: It is an immodest dance, Mam'selle. Your arm around the waist of your partner indeed!

LAURA: But *your* arm doesn't count, Madame. If you were Captain Field now . . .

PERRODON breaks away from her.

PERRODON: Mam'selle Laura! Who puts such thoughts into your head?

LAURA: No one puts them there. They just come. One-two-three. One-two-three. In another week Cousin Beth will be here. Everyone in Paris dances the waltz. Cousin Beth said so when she wrote. You wouldn't want her to think us country bumpkins, would you? I'm sure she waltzes with the captain.

PERRODON: The waltz may be all very well for Paris, but France is on the other side of the world.

LAURA: Not quite.

PERRODON: Far enough. Here in Styria we are more— more ...

LAURA: Behind the times?

PERRODON: You should be thankful for what you have, child. Here you live in a castle. In Paris you would be confined to an apartment that would fit into our chapel— and still leave room over.

LAURA: Oh, I'm not complaining, Madame. Only trying to dance. Papa may have taught the servants Sir Roger de Coverley, but it lacks ...

PERRODON: One-two-three?

LAURA: One-two-three.

The music runs down and stops. LAURA *pauses too.*

LAURA: Cousin Beth is very pretty and very accomplished. You don't suppose she'll find me dull?

PERRODON: You are quite pretty enough, Laura, dear. And I have taught you all that it is necessary for a young lady to know.

LAURA: Except the waltz. Wind up the musical box again. One-two-three. One-two-three ...

She almost whirls into COLONEL SMITHSON. *Although British the colonel served in the Austrian army. He almost over-emphasises the fact that he still considers himself an English gentleman.*

He might have had something to say about the dancing lesson, but at present he has something else on his mind.

LAURA *waits for him to say something, but he is silent.*

LAURA: Papa?

SMITHSON: Bad news, I'm afraid.

LAURA: That letter?

SMITHSON (*realising that he is still holding it*): It came only a short while ago. From Paris.

LAURA: Cousin Beth? Oh, don't say she has postponed her visit again.

SMITHSON: You'll not be seeing your cousin, my dear. This year—or ever. Your uncle says that she—three weeks ago . . . It takes so long for a confounded letter to reach us here.

LAURA: What—happened?

SMITHSON: Your uncle writes—"I have lost my darling daughter. During the last days of dear Beth's illness I was not able to write to you. She died in the peace of innocence and in the glorious hope of a blessed futurity."

LAURA: Oh, Papa! Poor Beth. Let me see the letter.

SMITHSON: Better not, my dear. It contains—other details.

LAURA: Papa, please.

SMITHSON: It is for your own good. I wouldn't wish you to be—distressed.

LAURA: I can hardly be more distressed than I am now, Papa. Only a few weeks ago she wrote in the best of health and spirits.

SMITHSON: Her illness was apparently swift and fatal. Doctors could do nothing as she—slipped away. She suffered no pain. She fell asleep and did not wake again . . . I think now it would be best if you went to your room, and . . . I'll be writing to your uncle later today. If you wish to enclose a few lines.

LAURA: I'll do it at once . . . Oh, Madame, I was dancing. Dancing! I shall never dance again.

She runs from the room.

PERRODON: Poor young lady. But there is worse news in the letter, Colonel.

SMITHSON: H'm?

PERRODON: That you would not permit Mademoiselle Laura to read.

SMITHSON: There are some things it's better she shouldn't know about. I don't know what to make of it, I'm sure. He seemed such a reliable young feller. Not that I ever met him, of course, but the family thought highly of him. Promising career: sound stock . . .

PERRODON: Young man, Colonel?

SMITHSON: Was to have married my niece. Seems the shock drove him out of his mind. Don't know what the young men are coming to. God knows I suffered when my wife died. But the cure for that is work—not this hysterical nonsense. He's disappeared. Posted as a deserter by now, I shouldn't wonder. Couldn't face the accusations.

PERRODON: Accusations, Colonel?

SMITHSON: The day after the funeral he was seen leaving the cemetery at dawn. Later the coffin was found to have been disturbed. Somebody had driven a stake through the dead girl's heart. It must have been him. But why, in Heaven's name? Why?

He strides to the window and glares out, hating to admit that he is out of his depth.

PERRODON: Grief can get the better of a man, Colonel.

SMITHSON: He was a soldier, ma'am. He'd no right to let anything get the better of him . . . Good, God! Look at that.

His attention is attracted by something he sees through the window.

Galloping horses can be heard in the distance.

SMITHSON: The coachman's a lunatic. He'll never take the curve at that speed. He'll have the carriage over. And he's driving too close to the trees. There it goes.

The sound of hooves becomes the sound of frantic neighing.

SMITHSON: They could all be killed. (*Runs to the door.*) Call the servants. Fritz. Karl! (*Turns to* PERRODON.) See that Miss Laura stays in her room. May be a messy business down there. (*Strides out shouting.*) Johann. Rudi! Where are those men?

MADAME PERRODON *hurries to the window*.

PERRODON: Oh, les pauvres! Oh. Oh. Oh.

She hurries out after the colonel.

ACT ONE

Scene Three

THE DRAWING-ROOM

SMITHSON *strides into the room ahead of* IVAN.

SMITHSON: This way, man. The horses took fright, you say. I'd say the coachman was driving 'em too hard.

IVAN: A wheel caught the root of a tree, sir. The coachman could do nothing. But the carriage has been righted. It has suffered no more than scratches, and is ready to continue the journey.

SMITHSON: Which is more than can be said for the occupants.

IVAN: The young lady was the only one to be hurt, sir.

SMITHSON: As yet we don't know how badly. She's still unconscious.

IVAN: I hope you will pardon my speaking on behalf of my mistress, sir, but you will have seen her: she speaks neither English, French, nor German. She begs your pardon, too, but believes you will understand better if I carry her message.

SMITHSON: Go on. Go on.

IVAN: The journey which she has undertaken is a matter of life and death. To lose even one hour means possibly to lose everything. The young lady will not recover for—how long? My mistress cannot—dare not—delay. Affairs of state, you understand, lie in the balance. So the young lady must be left behind.

SMITHSON: The devil she must!

IVAN: My mistress asks that you would be kind enough to convey her daughter to the nearest village. There must be an inn where the young lady can stay for a month or so until my mistress returns.

SMITHSON: Nonsense.

IVAN: You refuse, sir?

SMITHSON: We'll look after the young lady here.

IVAN: I'm not sure, sir . . .

SMITHSON: She'll be in good hands. I was a colonel in the Austrian Service. Your mistress can check on my credentials when she has leisure. And my daughter has an excellent Swiss governess.

IVAN: That was not my meaning, sir. It is most chivalrous of you; but we could not impose . . .

SMITHSON: No imposition at all. To tell the truth your mistress might be doing us a favour. My daughter has just suffered a cruel disappointment. It would be good for her to have a companion for the next few weeks.

IVAN: You know nothing of us, sir.

SMITHSON: I noticed the coat of arms on the carriage. I wouldn't recommend our village for the young lady. It would prove rougher lodging than she must be used to. No, your mistress may leave her daughter here. She'll be cared for.

IVAN: I am sure my mistress will arrange for you to be suitably compensated.

SMITHSON: Compensated, man? Damnit, I'm not an innkeeper. It's no more than would be expected of a gentleman.

IVAN: Nevertheless you will accept the thanks of my mistress, sir.

SMITHSON: Yes, yes, yes. You'd best be getting back to the carriage if her affairs are as urgent as you suggest.

IVAN: At once, sir.

Clicks his heels and gives a slight bow.

As he turns to leave he meets PERRODON coming into the room.

He makes a slight bow to her then continues out.

SMITHSON: The Countess's servant, Madame. I don't applaud her choice. And he's the best of a wild-looking bunch. Has Spielsberg been sent for?

PERRODON: He should be here in an hour or so, Colonel.

SMITHSON *crosses to the window.*

SMITHSON: The girl still unconscious?

PERRODON: I left her with a cold bandage on her head.

SMITHSON: It's a responsibility, but there was nothing else I . . .

PERRODON: She looks a poor, delicate thing.

SMITHSON: Yes, well . . . There was nothing I could . . . Affairs of state, he said. A child of that age shouldn't be mixed up in . . . Far better for her to stay here.

LAURA *has come into the room.*

LAURA: Who. Papa? What has been happening? The servants ran past my room chattering like magpies.

SMITHSON: There was an accident by the main gate.

LAURA (*running to the window*): Where? What happened?

SMITHSON: Nothing for you to worry about, my dear. A coach overturned.

LAURA: Why wasn't I told?

SMITHSON: There was no telling how unpleasant the details may have been. Blood and broken bones maybe.

LAURA: Really, Papa. I'm not a child. I'm not.

SMITHSON: So you say, dear. Some things in life have to be faced when they happen; but until then I'd rather you were protected.

LAURA: I cannot always be protected, Papa.

SMITHSON: We'll see about that. There's no need to pull a face. You should be thankful you're not abandoned among strangers like that other child.

LAURA: What other child?

SMITHSON: At a minute's notice.

LAURA: Madame Perrodon, you tell me. What happened?

PERRODON (*uncertain what to say with the Colonel there*): Well—your papa . . .

SMITHSON: There was nothing else I could have done.

PERRODON: You are to have a new companion for a while, mademoiselle.

LAURA: Companion?

SMITHSON: Yes, her name is—er—is . . . Madame, her name.

PERRODON: Her name?

SMITHSON: It's—er . . .

CARMILLA (*in a whisper that fills the room*): Carmilla.

They all turn to see CARMILLA *in the doorway.*

She is a girl of about nineteen, dark and pale, her speech and movements are languid, but not like a person who is ill, rather like someone in a dream.

LAURA *stares at her as though hypnotised.*

LAURA: You!

CARMILLA (*with the same intensity*): You!

She holds out her arms, takes another step towards LAURA, *then faints.*

ACT ONE

Scene Four

THE DRAWING-ROOM

CARMILLA *stands by the window. She turns as* SMITHSON *enters with* DOCTOR SPIELSBERG. SPIELSBERG *is coldly professional. He is not a typical country doctor.*
He is as elegantly fastidious as he can afford, and is as out of place in these surroundings as hob-nailed boots would be in Vienna.

SMITHSON: This is Doctor Spielsberg.

The DOCTOR *gives a slight bow.*

CARMILLA (*drifting towards him*): My name is Carmilla.

DOCTOR: A charming and unusual name.

CARMILLA: It's of no importance.

DOCTOR: The Colonel's messenger battered at my door with such fury I hardly expected to discover my patient on her feet.

CARMILLA: I was not consulted before the servant was despatched—otherwise I would have advised against it.

SMITHSON: You were unconscious, young lady.

CARMILLA: I have a headache, which is only to be expected—but nothing worse.

DOCTOR: That's to be seen. As I'm here, an examination . . .

CARMILLA (*smiling*): You wish to earn your fee, Doctor.

DOCTOR: The fee is immaterial, young lady. I wish to allay Colonel Smithson's anxiety. His guest must have every attention.

CARMILLA: You are most kind, Colonel.

SMITHSON: Anything that I can . . . I'll leave you, Spielsberg, to get on with the examination.

DOCTOR: It should not take long, Colonel.

SMITHSON *leaves the room.*

CARMILLA: Now you expect to count my heartbeats and check my temperature.

DOCTOR: Usual preliminaries.

CARMILLA: You should not become a slave to habit, Doctor. (*She returns to the window.*) Put away your instruments.

DOCTOR (*putting her in her place*): My dear young lady . . .

CARMILLA (*turning to face him*): Young lady?

After a few seconds of her gaze, the DOCTOR *turns away, put out.*

Doctor (*haltingly*): Permit me to—know—what is best for you.

Carmilla: You have my word, Doctor. Your stethoscope and thermometer would detect nothing.

Doctor: If you'll pardon my insistence, young lady—Fräulein Carmilla—I have the evidence of my eyes. You are ill.

Carmilla: The journey was long and rough. I am tired that is all.

Doctor: Nevertheless I must insist . . .

Carmilla (*with a sudden flash of anger*): It is I who insist, Doctor! (*Lapsing into her customary languor again.*) I have offended you. Please forgive me.

Doctor: In certain matters you must allow your physician some discretion.

Carmilla: My short life has been a cosmopolitan one. The Countess, my mother . . .

Doctor: Countess?

Carmilla: My mother travels much. For the moment I forgot that I was in a remote part of the Styrian mountains.

Doctor: Then this uncouth leech reminded you that you had ben cast away in a rustic wilderness.

Carmilla: Would a country doctor's hands be so perfectly manicured? Would a country doctor's coat be so fashionably cut, his cravat so impeccably tied. For a moment I imagined myself in Vienna.

Doctor: Flattery is always welcome—even when one knows it is flattery. I took my degree in Vienna. For a while I lived on hopes. Then I returned to these clods.

Carmilla: To these forests. They scent the breeze. I have never been in these parts before, but I expect the girls are strong and lusty, the red blood glowing in their cheeks. Here I shall become as healthy as one of your milkmaids. And you shall claim the credit, Doctor Spielsberg.

Some distance away LAURA *can be heard calling "Papa".*

CARMILLA: Is the examination over?

DOCTOR: What am I to tell the Colonel?

CARMILLA: What would you have said if you were in Vienna?

LAURA *runs in holding a small portrait.*

LAURA: Papa, look at . . . Oh, I beg your pardon, Doctor.

She glances shyly at CARMILLA, *who is looking at her with a fixed intensity.*

LAURA: I'll return later.

CARMILLA: Don't go. The doctor has finished. He has no more interest in me.

DOCTOR: You are mistaken, Fräulein. I shall continue to take an interest in you.

LAURA: Is the Fräulein feeling better?

CARMILLA: Please—Carmilla.

LAURA (*still shyly, feeling all hands and feet in the presence of this sophisticated creature*): Carmilla. (*Suddenly holds out the picture.*) Look. I had to search the lumber room for it. But look. It's you.

CARMILLA *merely glances at the picture, then returns her gaze to* LAURA.

CARMILLA: Is it?

DOCTOR: May I? (*He takes the picture from* LAURA.)

LAURA (*enthusiastically*): Everything about it is Carmilla—the eyes, the mouth, the hair. Even—yes—even that small mole on your neck.

DOCTOR: An excellent likeness.

LAURA: Except that it is not Carmilla. There is writing in gold at the bottom of the picture. The letters are faded, but . . .

DOCTOR (*holding it up to the light*): Marcia—Countess Karnstein—1698.

LAURA: Isn't that amazing?

DOCTOR: Of course you are descended from the Karnsteins, young lady.

LAURA: At least, Mama was.

DOCTOR: Which explains how the picture came to be here in the castle. But the likeness . . .

CARMILLA: I believe I am descended from the Karnsteins, too. A very long descent.

LAURA: You must have a talk with the doctor. He knows all about the family. He spends his spare time hunting through ancient records and tracing inscriptions on tombstones.

DOCTOR: Time lies heavily in a mountain village, and my hunting instincts were never directed towards animals.

LAURA: He'll be able to tell you exactly where . . .

CARMILLA: It's of no importance.

DOCTOR: Actually the name is not Marcia. The lettering is so faded but one can just see . . . Mircalla.

LAURA: Mircalla?

CARMILLA: Mircalla lies in her tomb. Carmilla is here with you.

DOCTOR: The Karnstein line is finished now. They were ruined in the Civil Wars long ago. The ruins of their castle stand about three miles away . . . Your picture, young lady. (*He hands it to* LAURA.) I'm surprised I hadn't seen it before. Your father produced the old documents. Strange that he should have overlooked the portrait.

LAURA: Oh, it happened about twelve years ago, Doctor. While you were still in Vienna.

DOCTOR: What—happened?

SMITHSON, *annoyed, strides into the room.*

SMITHSON: I gave orders for that picture to be put away.

LAURA: Surely there can be no harm now, Papa. I'm quite grown up.

SMITHSON (*not wanting an argument*): H'm . . . Ready to report, Doctor?

DOCTOR: There's nothing wrong with Fräulein Carmilla that a stay here may not cure. She needs fresh air, fresh vegetables, fresh meat, and eight hours' sleep at night.

CARMILLA: What if I cannot rest at night, Doctor?

DOCTOR: You will. Here you will.

SMITHSON: Good. Now I'd like you to look at one of the grooms. Seems to be developing some sort of abcess. Needs attention.

CARMILLA: Perhaps the doctor feels that you should have sent for a veterinary surgeon.

DOCTOR: I practise impartially. However I confess that I find conversation with a countess more stimulating than with a stable-boy. I shall return.

Gives a slight bow, and goes out closely followed by SMITHSON.

SMITHSON: The feller's been getting clumsier every day. He's only just admitted that . . .

CARMILLA *and* LAURA *are left together. They are*

strangers—but not strangers. Each waits for the other to make the first move.

LAURA: The—picture used to hang in my bedroom . . . I asked for it after Mama died . . . It reminded me a little of her.

CARMILLA: It was the last thing you saw when you went to sleep.

LAURA: That's what Doctor Baum said—he was our old doctor before Doctor Spielsberg came. He had some peculiar ideas. He believed the picture caused my bad dream.

CARMILLA: Bad—dream?

LAURA: They say I screamed and screamed. Everyone came running to my room.

CARMILLA: Your bedroom is wainscotted in dark wood. By the bed is a wrought iron candlestick with two branches Tall windows open on to the terrace, and in the distance you can see the ruined castle.

LAURA: You've seen my room, haven't you?

CARMILLA: One night when I was about eight years old, I awoke in a strange room. I heard someone crying, and when I looked towards the bed I saw a young lady. She had fair hair and blue eyes. It was you as you are now. She held out her arms and I climbed into bed with her. I think we both fell asleep. Suddenly she was sitting up in bed and screaming. I was frightened and slipped down to the ground. When I opened my eyes again I was in my nursery at home.

LAURA: It *was* you, then. It *was* you! It was not long after Mama died. I was crying myself to sleep when I saw the face from the picture at the side of my bed. She lay down beside me. Then I felt a pain as though two needles ran into my neck. I began to scream. I tried to explain to Papa what had happened but my room was empty. There was nothing to see on my neck, but I still remember the pain. Like two needles.

CARMILLA: I would never hurt you, Laura. I have never forgotten you.

LAURA: Could we have shared a dream?

CARMILLA: I knew that we must meet again.

LAURA: Papa took the picture away.

CARMILLA: But you found it.

LAURA: I went to look at it sometimes. (*She looks from the picture to* CARMILLA.) She—you . . . I can't understand. Who are you?

CARMILLA: My name is Carmilla.

LAURA: Where have you come from?

CARMILLA: I have come a long way, and I have a long way to go.

LAURA: Who are your family?

CARMILLA: I am alone. Terribly alone.

LAURA: But . . .

CARMILLA: And tired. Oh, so tired.

She sways, and LAURA *runs to her to support her.*

LAURA (*calling*): Madame Perrodon. Madame Perrodon . . . There. Put your arm round me. You should not have dismissed the doctor so lightly.

CARMILLA: I need no doctors. I need . . . I need . . . no doctor. But who would have guessed that I might find you here? In this place. Here.

MADAME PERRODON *hurries in.*

PERRODON: Ah. What has happened?

CARMILLA: It seems, madame, that I have less strength than I imagined.

PERRODON: The doctor is here still. I'll send for him.

CARMILLA: No, not the doctor. I need only sleep, I promise. I shall be better in the morning.

PERRODON: I'll brew my special tizanne. Now take my arm.

CARMILLA: You are so kind.

They walk a few steps, then CARMILLA *turns back to* LAURA.

CARMILLA: Laura, dare I ask for more? May I have the picture?

LAURA: I was about to ask Papa if I may hang it in my room again.

CARMILLA: The time to hang it in your room will be after I have gone. Until then do you need the picture?

LAURA *puts the portrait into* CARMILLA'S *hands.*

LAURA: Forgive me. I was forgetting . . . You are our guest.

CARMILLA: More than a guest, I hope. We shall be friends?

LAURA: We must. But I'm so confused.

CARMILLA: Everything will become clear in time. One day you will know everything. Goodnight my dear.

LAURA: Goodnight.

CARMILLA: And please—before you sleep—think of me.

LAURA: I'll remember you in my prayers.

CARMILLA: In your prayers? Ah, yes. And after your prayers—in your dreams.

CARMILLA *goes out with* MADAME PERRODON. LAURA *is left alone.*

LAURA: My dreams?

ACT ONE

Scene Five

THE TERRACE OF THE CASTLE

LAURA stands alone in a shaft of moonlight. She shields her eyes against the brilliant light.

CARMILLA's voice whispers "Laura".

LAURA turns towards the direction of the voice.

LAURA: Who is there?

The whisper comes from a different direction—"Laura".

LAURA: Who is it? What do you want?

From yet another direction—"Laura".

LAURA spins round in her attempts to locate the source of the sound.

LAURA: Where are you?

The whisper merely replies—"Laura".

LAURA: I'm trying to find you, but I can't. You're everywhere. You're nowhere.

WHISPER: Laura.

LAURA: There you are.

She runs into the shadows.

WHISPER: Laura.

LAURA: There.

She runs in the opposite direction, trying to catch the whisperer.

LAURA: Come out. Come out.

WHISPER: Laura.

LAURA: I *shall* find you. I shall.

WHISPER: Laura.

LAURA runs in the direction of the whisper.

She runs into a dark-cloaked figure which envelopes her in the cloak.

LAURA gives a frightened shriek.

Blackout.

In the darkness PERRODON's consoling voice can be heard.

PERRODON: There, there, ma petite. Don't be afraid. Perrodon is here.

LAURA: Madame Perrodon?

Slowly light returns—the cold grey light of dawn on the terrace of the castle.

PERRODON: Ah, the little one is awake now, n'est ce pas?

LAURA: Where am I? The terrace? Why should I be on the terrace?

PERRODON: You were walking in your sleep. Fortunately I heard . . .

LAURA: You heard? What did you hear?

PERRODON: Your footsteps, child. I followed you here. Now come inside before your papa wakes and worries.

LAURA: I was dreaming. Someone was calling to me. I was trying to find them, but I couldn't. I wanted to find them, but they were always just out of sight. It was—it was . . . I can't remember.

PERRODON: Ssh, now. Ssh.

In the distance a wolf howls.

LAURA: What was that?

PERRODON: A dog down in the village.

The wolf howls again.

LAURA: A wolf. In the forest.

PERRODON: Far enough, anyway. You're cold.

LAURA: I'm frightened.

The wolf howls.

LAURA: Deliver us from evil.

PERRODON: What is the child saying? There's nothing here to harm you. Now come back to bed, and I'll make you a cup of English tea.

The wolf howls.

LAURA: You were right. It is a long way off . . . You won't tell Papa, will you?—that you found me here. He would fret, and I don't want him to fret.

PERRODON: You go to sleep again, and by the time you wake up, everything will be forgotten. Come along.

The wolf howls.

LAURA: I've remembered now. The voice . . .

PERRODON: There was no voice. You were dreaming. Come, now.

As they go inside, the wolf howls.

ACT ONE

Scene Six

THE TERRACE

SMITHSON *strides out into bright sunshine.*

SMITHSON: Out here, Spielsberg.

The DOCTOR *follows him.*

SMITHSON: Bright and early, eh? Bright and early.

DOCTOR: I should have arrived sooner, but I was detained in the village. Pure routine, but it had to be attended to. Now they can get on with the funeral.

SMITHSON: Funeral?

DOCTOR: The daughter of one of the rangers. A week ago the girl was running about. Tomorrow she'll be buried.

SMITHSON: Hopeless case?

DOCTOR: That is the polite assumption, Colonel. As usual I was called in too late—barely in time to certify the cause of death.

SMITHSON: Which was?

DOCTOR: Officially fever. In point of fact inadequate diet, absurd hygiene, and lethal sanitation. Education is the only cure and we may not achieve that for centuries. They cling to their charms and their conjurings. They dabble their fingers in holy water when they should be scrubbing their hands with disinfectant. I beg your pardon: I don't often mount my hobby-horse. I take it you're more concerned with the progress of your own patient.

SMITHSON: I still don't care for that pallor.

DOCTOR: I find it attractive.

SMITHSON: She's as weak as a kitten, and she picks at her food like a fasting canary. How can she expect to improve when she don't eat?

DOCTOR: But she is improving, Colonel. You must give our mountain air time to work its cure. Believe me she is much stronger. Look.

SMITHSON: She's still leaning on my daughter's arm.

DOCTOR: But not, I think, for physical support.

SMITHSON: H'm?

DOCTOR: At this distance one would take them for sisters —one dark and one fair, but still sisters.

SMITHSON: They took to each other immediately. In many ways it was a lucky accident. Laura needed company. She'd been expecting her cousin, poor girl. Told you about that, didn't I? Wasting disease. Very sad. Then this one comes crashing out of the forest.

DOCTOR: I'm sure the villagers can provide a local superstition to account for her timely appearance.

CARMILLA *enters, leaning on the arm of* LAURA.

CARMILLA: Good morning, Doctor. Have you persuaded the Colonel that I may live after all?

DOCTOR: Take enough fresh air and fresh meat, and you'll survive to be a hundred.

CARMILLA: Do you take your own advice, Doctor? Will you report to me on your hundredth birthday?

LAURA: We walked almost to the edge of the forest this morning.

SMITHSON: Take care of our guest, my dear. Mustn't overtax her.

CARMILLA: I have found here, Colonel, all that I need to recover my strength.

SMITHSON: Maybe so. But you mustn't try to compete with my daughter in running and climbing.

LAURA: Papa! You make me sound a hobbledehoy.

CARMILLA: One day soon you shall see what I am capable of. I should like to visit the ruins of Karnstein. Am I permitted to walk as far as the castle?

DOCTOR: Three miles?

CARMILLA: Is it so far? It seems so near from my window. So grim. So romantic.

LAURA: We could drive there in the carriage, couldn't we, Papa?

SMITHSON: One of these days.

LAURA: Doctor Spielsberg could come with us, too. Then he need have no fears about his patient.

SMITHSON: Spielsberg has work to do.

DOCTOR: Time can always be found for important engagements. I shall be delighted to accompany the ladies when they command. But, as the Colonel says, I have other patients. Will you accompany me, sir, as far as the stables?

SMITHSON: Was just about to suggest it.

The DOCTOR *leaves with* SMITHSON.

CARMILLA: Sometimes I feel Spielsberg knows more than he says.

LAURA: All doctors do. To tell the truth I have always found Doctor Spielsberg rather forbidding; but in your company he seems to blossom.

CARMILLA: To him I am "an interesting case". I have known many doctors.

LAURA: Were you very ill?

CARMILLA: More than you have ever been—or ever can be but once.

LAURA: Was it long ago?

CARMILLA: Very long ago. So long ago that it seems almost a dream. For a while I forgot everything but pain and weakness.

LAURA: But you recovered.

CARMILLA: I am here.

LAURA: Papa was right, though. I mustn't overtire you. You must forgive me sometimes if I seem to run ahead, but I

have never been ill. Not really ill. You *will* tell me
when you feel tired, won't you? Perhaps we should go in
now.

CARMILLA: No, my dear. Stay here with me.

LAURA: Is the sun too bright for you?

CARMILLA: I heard a cry in the night. Was it your voice,
Laura?

LAURA: Shall I fetch a parasol for you?

CARMILLA: Did you have a bad dream?

LAURA: I wouldn't want you to become ill again.

CARMILLA: I can never suffer *that* sickness again. Laura, did
you hear a cry last night?

LAURA: I heard nothing. At least—a wolf, perhaps. Wolves
have been seen near the deserted village.

CARMILLA: I opened my window. I thought I saw someone
on the terrace.

LAURA: I saw no one. I was asleep.

CARMILLA: And dreaming?

LAURA: Perhaps.

CARMILLA: What did you dream?

LAURA: I can never remember dreams. Now you must sit
down.

CARMILLA: Were you so anxious to forget?

LAURA: I'll fetch a cushion.

CARMILLA: Laura.

She grasps LAURA's *wrist.* LAURA *stops dead, turns slowly,
and looks down at* CARMILLA's *hand.*

LAURA (*perplexed*): Your hand. It grips like steel.

CARMILLA *releases her.*

CARMILLA (*with a slight laugh*): I warned you that I am stronger than the doctor will admit.

LAURA *thoughtfully rubs her wrist.*

CARMILLA: I didn't hurt you, did I? I promised I would never hurt you.

LAURA: No, you didn't hurt me. For the moment you almost frightened me.

CARMILLA: There is nothing to fear, my dear. Nothing.

She puts her arm around LAURA's *shoulder.*

There is a sudden cacophany nearby. A tambourine is rattled and a voice that should belong to a Punch and Judy show sings a few lively bars.

CARMILLA *draws back from* LAURA.

CARMILLA: Who is there?

Still singing and beating the tambourine a hunchbacked mountebank appears. He is dressed in a medley of brightly coloured rags, with the apparatus of his profession tied and strapped all over him. There is a box hanging on his left side, a satchel on his right side, and a pack on his back. His hair is covered by a gay cap, and a black beard covers most of his face. There is a glove puppet on his right hand, and this appears to beat at the tambourine held in his left.

In fact there is little to suggest that under the ribbons and bells is CAPTAIN FIELD.

FIELD: Buon giorno, signorine.

He makes an extravagant bow. When he speaks it is with an Italian accent.

FIELD: I pleasa the signorine, eh? I gotta plenty to make laugh, eh?

CARMILLA: What is this—a one man circus?

FIELD: Notta one man. I gotta hassistance. This Beppo.

He holds up the glove puppet.

FIELD: Ver clever Beppo. He catch. (*He tosses the tambourine which the puppet catches.*) He throw. (*He catches the tambourine again.*) He play tambourine. (*The puppet beats at the tambourine.*) He bow. (*The puppet bows.*) You no clap when he play tambourine? Beppo disappoint. He hide head.

LAURA: Poor Beppo.

FIELD: Ah! Look atta young lady, Beppo. (*The puppet raises its head then quickly hides again.*) No, no, no.

LAURA *laughs.*

FIELD: I tell Beppo a secret. (*Whispers in puppet's ear. The puppet looks up.*) H'm? . . . Si. (*Puppet looks at* LAURA, *then hides its head again.*) No . . . Come, Beppo. Shake hands with the young lady. (*Coyly the puppet edges towards* LAURA.) That's a right. Shake hands.

Suddenly the puppet sticks out its hand. Solemnly LAURA *shakes it.*

As though wearied by this childishness CARMILLA *drifts away.*

FIELD: Beppo say "How do?" (*He watches* CARMILLA *as she stands with her back rather ostentatiously turned towards him.*) Once I have real monkey. My little Beata. I love Beata: Beata love me. But she die. She get sick. In one—two—three day she dead.

Slowly CARMILLA *turns to stare at him.*

LAURA: I'm so sorry.

FIELD (*briskly*): But the signorine no wanta sad story. Whata then? I stand on my head while I play fiddle. No? I cura wart. But you no gotta wart to cure. I sing again, no?

LAURA (*laughing*): No, thank you.

FIELD: I gotta bead an' necklace in my box. You lika bead. Genuine ruby.

LAURA: No, thank you.

FIELD: I show you what I got. (*He fumbles in his box and brings out a slip of paper with cabbalistic scrawls on it.*)

LAURA: What on earth . . . ?

FIELD: Lucky charm. Maka you sleep sweet. No bad dream.

LAURA: I—I don't have bad dreams.

FIELD: Keep away all evil. Keep away the oupire.

LAURA: The oupire?

FIELD: All round here nothing but story of oupire. La ragazza in the village. She see it. Today she phtt!

LAURA: Dead?

FIELD: I justa come from down there. Sell lotsa these today.

LAURA: I hadn't heard about it.

FIELD: The doctor he shake his head. Too late, he say. She shoulda bought charm sooner.

LAURA: Perhaps . . .

CARMILLA: Don't waste your money.

FIELD: The younga lady need protection from the oupire.

CARMILLA: Scrawls on paper never protected anyone.

FIELD: It notta the scrawl—these scrawl all genuine mind—but it's the faith. You believe these paper keep away evil, then these paper damnwell keep away evil. Scusa.

CARMILLA: Do you believe that you can buy faith?

LAURA (*reluctantly*): No.

FIELD: The signorina no buy?

LAURA (*fumbling in a purse*): But you deserve something for the entertainment. Here. Take this for Beppo.

She drops a coin into the box.

FIELD: An Beppo give you this becausa he like the young lady who shaka hand.

The puppet holds out one of the charms.

LAURA: No, I don't really . . .

FIELD: Per favore. For Beppo.

LAURA: Well—thank you. (*She takes the charm*).

FIELD: Prego. Pin to your pillow and you laugh at any oupire that ever was.

LAURA: But I've never heard of this oupire. What is it?

FIELD: Evil . . . But I notta done nothing for the other signorina.

CARMILLA: I have charms of my own. More potent than your shreds of paper.

FIELD: I gotta more talent than plenty. Ecco—dentista.

LAURA: But my friend doesn't need a dentist.

FIELD: I have the seeing eye. La contessa has the tooth. Long and thin like the needle. Ha? With my long sight as she stand here I see it distinct. Now I think it hurt the young lady. So . . . I have the file, the punch and the nippers. I maka the tooth round and blunt. Heh? Mi permetta?

CARMILLA (*trying to control her temper*): Get away from here. Never let me see you again.

LAURA: Why Carmilla . . .

CARMILLA: Does your father allow his guests to be insulted by mountebanks?

LAURA: He was only trying to ...

CARMILLA (*her temper getting the better of her*): At home I would have his back laid open at the cart tail.

FIELD (*cringing*): Mi dispiace.

CARMILLA (*shouting*): I would have your slandering tongue cut out.

FIELD: Perdona. Sono disgraziato.

LAURA: Carmilla!

CARMILLA *suddenly realises where she is. She puts her hand to her head and sways.*

LAURA *runs to her.*

CARMILLA: My head. It swims.

LAURA: Let me help you inside. Oh, it's my fault. I shouldn't have taken you so far. I shouldn't have allowed you to stay in the sun. Take my arm. I'll call Madame Perrodon. (*To* FIELD *as they pass.*) Go, please. Go quickly. I'm sorry, but ...

CARMILLA: Absurd that a fool should make one into a fool.

LAURA: There. There. You were tired. Now what will Papa say?

FIELD *watches them go.*

When they are out of sight he straightens as far as his disguise and paraphernalia will allow.

He begins to laugh.

FIELD: The young lady has the long tooth.

In the distance a bell begins to toll.

FIELD's *laughter is cut short.*

He walks away.

As he does so the light fades and the bell grows louder.

ACT ONE

Scene Seven

THE KARNSTEIN RUINS

Dappled daylight filters through the ruined roof of what was once the chapel of the Karnstein Castle.

CARMILLA and LAURA can be heard laughing off, as the DOCTOR assists MADAME PERRODON over the rough ground.

DOCTOR: If Madame will take care over these stones.

PERRODON: So untidy.

DOCTOR: The rains fall, the winds blow, and down come the castle walls.

PERRODON: This tangle of weeds. Someone should clear them.

DOCTOR: There is no one here but the noble dead. They don't complain at the nettles and hemlock.

CARMILLA and LAURA come in laughing. CARMILLA has lost much of her langour, but she still holds LAURA's arm.

DOCTOR: Welcome to the home of the Karnsteins. Somewhat in need of repair, I fear. But there is grandeur even in ruin.

CARMILLA (*looking around her*): Yes, it is different now.

LAURA: Different?

CARMILLA: I have seen it only from my window, remember. It is very different inside.

LAURA: I hope you are not disappointed.

CARMILLA: Oh, no. How still it is.

DOCTOR: The villagers avoid the place. Neither threats nor bribes would bring one of them here. So the Karnsteins will rest undisturbed until Judgement Day.

CARMILLA: All of them?

DOCTOR: Most of them. Even those killed pillaging their neighbours were brought back to the Karnstein stronghold.

CARMILLA: Is the Countess—what was her name?

DOCTOR: Mircalla.

CARMILLA: Does she lie here?

DOCTOR: Almost certainly.

CARMILLA: Where?

DOCTOR: I have more work to do before I am absolutely sure. There are one or two tombs whose occupants are in doubt. But I shall solve the riddle.

CARMILLA: I should like to see her resting place—the one who looked so like me.

DOCTOR: So you shall before you leave.

PERRODON: Morbid pleasures.

LAURA: I don't like this place, either.

CARMILLA: Why was a whole village allowed to fall into decay, Doctor?

DOCTOR: The usual story. An epidemic decimated the population, so they moved to healthier ground. As soon as the ground was left to itself, brambles and ivy took over. Afterwards legends sprang up like the weeds.

CARMILLA: What legends, Doctor?

DOCTOR: There are enough monsters in the folk-lore of this district to populate a fairy-story book. The locals are quite capable of frightening themselves to death. And they infect one another with their superstitions.

LAURA: I can understand their fears. I could imagine . . .

PERRODON: That you must not do, ma petite. We want no more bad dreams.

LAURA looks a warning at her, the DOCTOR a question, and CARMILLA smiles a fleeting knowing smile.

PERRODON: I mean such a place must give rise to bad dreams. I intend to walk outside in the sunlight.

CARMILLA: There is sunlight here, Madame.

PERRODON: And even more shadows. Come, Laura.

As she turns to go she stumbles. The DOCTOR puts out a hand to steady her.

DOCTOR: My arm, Madame. You do the chapel less than justice. It is elegantly proportioned.

CARMILLA: Laura. (*She puts out a restraining hand towards* LAURA.)

PERRODON: I have not been here more than three times in the last eighteen years, and I do not care if this is the last.

CARMILLA: Stay, Laura.

PERRODON: I am sure there must be snakes here.

DOCTOR: Not snakes, Madame.

PERRODON: Spiders, then.

She and the DOCTOR move out of earshot.

LAURA: Why did you want to stay behind? It smells of decay.

CARMILLA: And that disturbs you? It reminds me of

crumbling timbers, softly flaking into dust. And dust settling like snow into a thick, silencing carpet.

LAURA: It reminds me of a grave.

CARMILLA: Yet I think you will come to love it as I do.

LAURA: Love it? I hate this place.

CARMILLA: Hate, little one? You only hate because you do not understand.

LAURA: Everywhere there is the smell of death. Madame was right. Only the dead belong here with the dead.

She makes to follow PERRODON, *but* CARMILLA *is standing in her way.*

CARMILLA: One day you will join them.

LAURA: Not here.

CARMILLA: Death comes to everyone. He is stronger than anyone else in the world. Even these great arches crumbled before him. Why struggle against him? Although he is all powerful, his touch is softer than a lover's.

LAURA: I don't know what you're talking about. Now come with me.

CARMILLA (*holding her back with the lightest touch on her arm*): Make peace with death and you share his strength.

LAURA: Please...

CARMILLA: Death unites everyone. There is no parting in death.

LAURA: I don't want to think about it.

CARMILLA: We shall be together for ever.

LAURA: We?

CARMILLA: You are mine. You shall be mine.

LAURA: I don't know you when you look and talk so.

She backs away from CARMILLA.

CARMILLA *puts her hand to her head.*

CARMILLA: What is the matter? You're like a frightened bird. What have I been saying?

LAURA: You—don't know?

CARMILLA: Where are the others? When did they go? It's this terrifying weakness. I thought I had conquered it. One minute I can race with you, and next minute I'm tottering like a child . . . Something has happened. I put out my hand to you here—then suddenly you seemed to disappear.

LAURA *runs back to her.*

LAURA: Poor Carmilla!

CARMILLA: I did not sleep well last night. I heard your wolves. Or perhaps I dreamed about them.

LAURA: You should have taken one of the charms from the mountebank. Since I pinned it to my pillow there have been no more bad dreams. If he should come again . . .

CARMILLA: I should still refuse to touch his amulets. I should despise myself for trusting in his scraps of paper.

LAURA: You may be right. But you won't despise me for keeping mine, will you?

CARMILLA: Keep it as long as you will, my dear. As the mountebank said—if you believe it will keep you from harm, maybe it will.

From a distance MADAME PERRODON *calls "Laura".*

LAURA: Madame Perrodon.

CARMILLA: Go to her.

LAURA: If you are not well, I must help you.

CARMILLA: No. Tell her that I shall follow in a moment. I should rather walk by myself. Then they will believe that I am getting better. And please don't mention my dizziness.

LAURA: Very well.

PERRODON (*off*): Laura.

LAURA: I am coming, Madame.

She walks away.

CARMILLA: Oh, Laura . . . Do you count it a bad dream when you dream of me?

LAURA *merely smiles and walks away.*

Left alone CARMILLA *takes a piece of paper from her bodice. It is the mountebank's amulet.*

She tears it to pieces and scatters the fragments.

CARMILLA: Now dream of me.

ACT ONE

Scene Eight

THE KARNSTEIN RUINS

CARMILLA *is now in the same position as at the end of the preceeding scene, but is now bathed in a fantastic light. She raises her arms and music begins— a distorted waltz.*

CARMILLA (*in an amplified whisper*): Laura. Laura.

LAURA *enters, walking as though in a trance. She curtsies low before* CARMILLA.

CARMILLA *holds out her hand, and* LAURA *kisses it.*

CARMILLA *raises up* LAURA.

CARMILLA: You are a Kranstein. You belong here with me.

LAURA: I belong.

CARMILLA: You have been chosen.

LAURA: I have been chosen.

CARMILLA: But you must make your choice.

LAURA: Make my choice.

CARMILLA: A mayfly's life or immortality.

LAURA: Immortality.

CARMILLA: Would you conquer death? Then embrace death. Would you defy corruption? Then take on corruption. Would you become all-powerful? Then surrender. Give up your body that your body may be preserved. Free your spirit that our souls may be one. Not Laura. Not Carmilla. But Laura in Carmilla. Surrender yourself.

LAURA: Surrender.

CARMILLA: Your blood.

LAURA: My blood.

Suddenly a huge bell begins to toll.

At the first boom CARMILLA *freezes.*

At the second boom the music becomes faster and faster and peters out in a whine.

At the third boom CARMILLA *puts her hands over her ears and screams.*

Blackout.

ACT ONE

Scene Nine

THE KARNSTEIN RUINS

Light slowly creeps in.

LAURA *lies huddled on the ground where she has fallen.*

In the distance a bell can be heard tolling.

The mountebank, without his impedimenta, runs up to LAURA *and kneels by her side.*

FIELD: Signorina. Signorina Laura. Svegliarsi. Wake up.

LAURA *stirs.*

LAURA: What?

FIELD: This is not good place for the signorina.

LAURA: What am I doing here?

FIELD: The signorina is—as we say—una somnambula.

LAURA: I walked in my sleep again?

FIELD: Si. That must be.

He helps her to her feet.

LAURA: But—why, these are the Karnstein ruins.

FIELD: No place for the signorina awake or asleep.

LAURA: There was a bell.

FIELD: Hark. She still ring. Over in the village. The village of the living—not lika this village.

LAURA: But why the bell?

FIELD: Another she die.

LAURA: Another?

FIELD: Now—cinque. Five die. This one ieri sera. Lasta night. Signorina—I beg—take care.

LAURA: I do. At least Madame Perrodon does.

FIELD: The Signora Perrodon she know, hah?

LAURA: At the first sign of a temperature she runs for the quinine.

FIELD: Medicine not so good for these fevers. You gotta the charm still? You pin to your pillow?

LAURA: It disappeared last night.

FIELD: She disappear, eh? I think I know where. (*Smacks his head.*) Now I no gotta one with me. But I got ... (*He tugs a small bunch of flowers from his belt.*) These flower.

LAURA: For me?

FIELD: Per favore. You keep in your room, eh? Very good against the sleepwalking—and other things. You take?

LAURA (*taking the flowers*): Thank you.

FIELD: I do more if I can. The bell stop now. But not long before it start again. Sei. Sette. Maybe more times before ...

LAURA: They'll be looking for me.

FIELD: Si. The Colonel he come. I think he follow me. Signorina, listen. Trust me. I trust you, but ...

He grasps her arms.

LAURA: What are you trying to tell me?

FIELD: I cannot tell too much. I cannot trust too much. But believe me the signorina must watch. Watch and pray.

LAURA: What a strange man you are.

FIELD: The signorina is too beautiful to die.

SMITHSON (*off*): You there. What the devil are you doing?

FIELD *releases* LAURA *and turns to face the angry Colonel who strides towards him.*

SMITHSON: Well?

LAURA: Papa ...

SMITHSON: I'm waiting, man. Your explanation.

FIELD: I follow the signorina.

SMITHSON: I know. The stable-boy saw you hanging round the gate.

FIELD: The signorina, she ...

LAURA: I was asleep, Papa.

SMITHSON: You walked three miles into the forest in your sleep?

FIELD: I wait 'till she wake. But I follow to make sure no harm come. There is much bad here.

SMITHSON: I see. You just happened to be by the castle at first light. You just happened to see my daughter leave. You just happened to know that she was walking in her sleep.

LAURA: But it's true, Papa.

SMITHSON (*baffled, but not knowing what to do*): H'm ... What have you got there? Throw them away, and come home.

FIELD: No!

SMITHSON: What?

LAURA: I picked them. I want to keep them in my room.

SMITHSON: Those? (*He looks from* FIELD *to* LAURA.) We'll talk about this later. Karl and Wilhelm are searching the other side of the track. (*He turns back to* FIELD.) If I were you, I'd avoid the castle in future.

FIELD: But signor ...

SMITHSON: The servants will have their orders.

He leads LAURA *away.*

FIELD *watches them go.*

DOCTOR (*off*): That was a warning. If I were you, I'd take notice.

FIELD *swings round to see* SPIELSBERG *approach*.

FIELD: What you do here?

DOCTOR: That's no concern of yours.

FIELD: You no want the Colonel to know.

DOCTOR: No matter. Tomorrow you will be gone.

FIELD: The tombs, eh? You looka for the old Countess. Where she lie, eh?

DOCTOR: You will pack your collection of cheats and tricks, and you will leave this district.

FIELD: Why you wanta me to go?

DOCTOR: Because to phrase the matter elegantly, you are a damned nuisance. You interfere.

FIELD: I no interfere, Dottore. You go back to your tombs. I no tell.

DOCTOR: The only persuasion you are likely to understand is a horse-whip to your hide. I'd use it now, only . . .

FIELD: We are alone, and lo sciocco might answer back.

DOCTOR: You are undermining my authority.

FIELD: No, Dottore. I help.

DOCTOR: What those peasants need is fresh air. Their windows and doors should be flung open to blow the pestilence away. I believed I had them convinced. But you pass down the street, and afterwards every crack is sealed, and what little air is left polluted with garlic.

FIELD: Garlic is good, Dottore. Oupire hate garlic.

DOCTOR: They are not alone. Fever is ravaging the village, and you . . .

FIELD: Not the fever, Dottore.

DOCTOR: Women are dying. Eight now.

FIELD: Otto.

DOCTOR: If you understand that better—otto. And another two are sick. They will die unless they come to their senses. And there is little chance of that while you peddle your amulets. I burned four of them yesterday.

FIELD: Then you have more patients waiting for you today.

DOCTOR: There'll come a time when you are sorry for your impertinence.

FIELD: I have journeyed far, Dottore. I have seen strange and terrible things.

DOCTOR: You'll se more if you stay here. I am told that our prison is very primitive, and very uncomfortable.

In the distance the bell begins to toll again.

DOCTOR (*involuntarily*): Lieber Gott!

FIELD: The bell.

DOCTOR: How the sound carries. It must be the morning breeze.

FIELD: Another. Still another.

DOCTOR: I suppose it *was* you who introduced that disgusting rite before the funeral.

FIELD: Rite?

DOCTOR: A stake through the heart of the corpse. Barbaric. Good day to you. I hope for your sake we shall not meet again.

FIELD *watches as the* DOCTOR *saunters away.*

FIELD (*without his accent*): I think we must, Doctor. I think we must.

He walks away in the opposite direction.

ACT ONE

Scene Ten

THE DRAWING-ROOM

LAURA, offstage, calls "Carmilla". She enters still holding her bunch of flowers. She looks about her and calls again.

Languidly and still smiling her half smile CARMILLA enters.

LAURA: Carmilla.

CARMILLA: My dear, everyone has been quite frantic for you—searching the castle from turret to cellar. Where have you been?

LAURA: You—didn't know?

CARMILLA: How could I? You slipped away before daybreak.

LAURA: You—didn't see me last night?

CARMILLA: Not after you kissed goodnight.

LAURA: It seemed so real. There were great banners round the walls, and the walls were so high that they disappeared up into the darkness. And there were shadows that were more than shadows.

CARMILLA: Poor Laura. You were dreaming again. If you were frightened by a nightmare, you should have called to me. I would have come to you.

LAURA: How could I call to you? You were there.

Smiling CARMILLA glides over towards LAURA, but stops short. She looks down at the flowers with disgust.

CARMILLA: What have you got there?

LAURA: Flowers.

CARMILLA: Throw them away.

LAURA: I thought they were pretty.

CARMILLA: Throw them away.

LAURA: Don't you like them?

CARMILLA (*backing away*): Evil things.

LAURA: These? They're wilted, but they'll recover in water.

CARMILLA: Burn them.

LAURA: I'll take them to my room.

CARMILLA: Your room?

LAURA: I promised him.

CARMILLA: Him?

LAURA: The mountebank. He said that they would keep the bad dreams away. I don't even know what they are.

CARMILLA: Brought up in the country, and you don't recognise wild garlic when you see it. Just the nosegay that gargoyle would pick. He reeks of garlic. He must be contaminated with it to the marrow of his bones.

LAURA: But these are so tiny, white, and harmless. Look.

Before CARMILLA *can react,* LAURA *has run over to her and thrust the flowers at her.*

The effect on CARMILLA *is devastating. She is almost paralysed. She gasps for air, and cannot speak.*

LAURA: Carmilla! The flowers? I'll throw them away.

She hurls the flowers away. They scatter over the floor.

LAURA: There. They've gone.

CARMILLA *slowly recovers.*

LAURA: I didn't realise they would make you ill.

CARMILLA: Never—never—bring such evil things—near me—again.

LAURA: I never shall.

CARMILLA: Evil. Evil.

LAURA: Please forgive me.

CARMILLA: There, there. I believe you are more distressed than I was. It's a foolish weakness, but I have learned to live with it.

LAURA: Last night the dream came again. She was—awe-inspiring. But she looked like you.

CARMILLA: Our ancestress, perhaps. The Countess.

LAURA: Why should I dream of her?

CARMILLA: Why should you dream of anything? Try to forget it.

LAURA: Most of it has faded already. I can only remember the great hall—and her—and the fact that I was about to do something terribly wrong. I knew it was wrong, but I had to do it. It was like being swept along by a flood.

CARMILLA: Next time you must surrender.

LAURA: Surrender?

CARMILLA: That is the only way you can break this dream. It will come again and again until you surrender to your desires. Give way to them. Who is to blame you? It is only a dream.

LAURA: I'm afraid.

CARMILLA: Because you fought the flood. Allow yourself to be carried with it.

LAURA: It could be evil.

CARMILLA: What do you know of evil, little one? You have yet to learn.

LAURA: To learn?

CARMILLA: I can teach you how to overcome your fears. If you are frightened tonight, call for me. I will come to you. And afterwards you shall come with me.

LAURA: With you?

CARMILLA: To death, through death, and beyond death.

LAURA: You are talking wild nonsense again.

CARMILLA: Very well, if you want me to leave you . . .

She walks a few steps towards the door, expecting LAURA to call her back. When no call comes, she pauses, and turns.

CARMILLA: You will call to me. You will. And I shall come to you.

She leaves LAURA.

LAURA stands alone and bewildered. She picks up the scattered flowers.

MADAME PERRODON bustles in.

PERRODON: Ah, there you are, cherie. Your papa is asking for you. He is pacing up and down the library and frowning.

LAURA: Will you put these in water for me?

She hands the flowers to PERRODON.

PERRODON: Poor things. They're half-dead.

LAURA: Flowers cannot be evil, can they?

PERRODON: These?

LAURA: Oh, Madame, why didn't you teach me to recognise evil?

PERRODON: What a suggestion! What should I know of evil? And what should you want to know?

She bustles out with the flowers.

LAURA *stands still.*

Slowly the light fades as the music of the waltz begins.

ACT ONE

Scene Eleven

THE DRAWING-ROOM

The music of the waltz grows, and is suddenly cut off as a shaft of light falls on LAURA, *standing alone.*

She puts out her hands as though the surrounding darkness were walls.

She turns round, trying to peer past the light.

LAURA: Where . . . ? Hello?

An echo repeats "LO LO LO LO".

LAURA: Papa.

Echo "PA PA PA PA".

LAURA: Carmilla.

This time the echo replies "Laura".

LAURA: Carmilla.

A cloaked and hooded figure glides through the shadows.

LAURA: Carmilla!

She takes a few steps towards the figure as though to embrace it, but the figure glides past her into the light. There it throws back the hood, and allowing the cloak to fall open, turns to face LAURA.

It is CARMILLA, but her dress is heavily splashed with blood, and blood trickles from her mouth.

LAURA screams and sways.

CARMILLA catches the fainting girl, and presses her mouth to LAURA's neck.

Blackout.

CURTAIN

ACT TWO

Scene One

THE DRAWING-ROOM

SMITHSON stands by the window, reading an official-looking report.

MADAME PERRODON hurries in.

PERRODON: Colonel Smithson...

SMITHSON (*without looking up*): H'm?

PERRODON: I should be most grateful if you would have words with the female servants.

SMITHSON (*looking up*): Me?

PERRODON: They may enjoy frightening themselves, but they must know where to draw the lines.

SMITHSON: I've responsibilities enough, Madame, without interfering with servants' gossip... If only Spielsberg knew how to write despatches.

PERRODON: I would speak to them myself, but I lack the authority.

SMITHSON: Nothing but a mess of ifs and buts. This is a time for facts—can act on facts—but he wastes half a page on drains.

PERRODON: Clara has frightened herself into hysterics.

SMITHSON: Ten dead, and Spielsberg babbles about sewage. Pardon the expression.

PERRODON: She swears the terrace is haunted.

SMITHSON: Give her a whiff of smelling salts and tell her to pull herself together.

PERRODON: Now they all recall seeing a white figure just before sunrise.

SMITHSON: Madame...

PERRODON: Not once, but several times.

SMITHSON: There is an outbreak of fever in the village. Do I, or do I not notify the authorities? By the side of that problem, servants foibles are insignificant.

PERRODON: I wish I could agree, Colonel.

SMITHSON: Spielsberg swears he can contain the epidemic. I take his point. If he succeeds, it's a feather in his cap. But if he don't there'll be awkward questions.

PERRODON: It is because of the sickness that the servants are spreading tales. They are saying it is not natural.

SMITHSON: Of course it's not natural. No fever's natural. The worst enemy a soldier has to face, and you can't even take cold steel to it. If only I could be certain of Spielsberg.

PERRODON: The doctor does his best. He seems always so assured.

SMITHSON: A good officer never admits the situation hopeless—even when he knows it. I expect a doctor to look assured. But I wish I knew what he's thinking. He hasn't even put a name to the thing. A wasting disease, he calls it. We can see that much for ourselves; but what disease is it that drains the life out of a girl in three days?

PERRODON: The servants declare it is no disease. They talk of spirits.

SMITHSON: At least we can forget that nonsense.

PERRODON: Things have been seen. Girls speak of being seized by the throat. There is talk of a figure in white. And the life is sucked from them.

SMITHSON: Better not speak of it here, Madame. We don't want the young ladies frightened. No more bad dreams and sleepwalking, huh? I'll have none of that idle prattling where Laura may hear it.

PERRODON: Then, Colonel, perhaps you had better speak to the servants.

SMITHSON (*sighing and folding up the report*): If I must. I'll give 'em something to be afraid of instead of their spooks.

As he turns to the door he realises that LAURA *has entered very quietly. She looks tired.*

SMITHSON: You crept in quietly, my dear.

LAURA: I was looking for Carmilla, Papa. I must speak to her.

PERRODON: What is the matter, cherie?

LAURA: She seems to have disappeared. Her room was empty this morning.

SMITHSON: I think Madame meant—what is the matter with you?

LAURA: Nothing, Papa. I feel tired, that is all.

SMITHSON: Tired?

SMITHSON *and* MADAME PERRODON *exchange worried glances.*

LAURA: I did not sleep well . . . Madame, the flowers were not in my room last night.

PERRODON: The poor things were as good as dead. I put roses there instead.

LAURA: I do not think roses . . . He said that I must . . . It doesn't matter. I must find Carmilla. Did she come to me? She could not. My room was locked. But her room was locked, too. Yet her room was empty.

SMITHSON: You're not talking sense, my dear.

LAURA: I'm sorry, Papa. I feel so confused.

PERRODON: Quinine, I think.

She crosses quickly to LAURA *and puts a hand on her head.*

LAURA: I am not ill, Madame. Only tired. I shall feel better in a while.

PERRODON: There is no fever, Colonel.

LAURA: Why should there be?

SMITHSON: Take care of her, Madame. She needs a rest.

LAURA: I wish you would not treat me as though I were sick, Papa. Just because I did not run all the way to this room . . . I must find Carmilla. If she has wandered into the forest . . .

SMITHSON: I'll have Karl and Wilhelm look for her. She can't be far away.

LAURA: Let me go with them. She could have gone to Karnstein. But why didn't she wait for me?

SMITHSON: Take your quinine like a good girl, and I'll do what can be done.

LAURA: Thank you, Papa. But why . . . ?

PERRODON: There is no need for you to worry, cherie. No need at all. Your papa will speak to the servants now.

She looks challengingly at SMITHSON.

SMITHSON: All the same . . . (*He glances at the report still in his hand.*) Confounded servants. Ghosts indeed!

He strides out bristling.

PERRODON: If you—felt—even a little ill, ma petite, you would tell Madame Perrodon?

LAURA: Of course.

PERRODON: There is—nothing you wish to tell me?

LAURA: No, Madame.

PERRODON: The Colonel is a good man, but not always the ideal confidante. There is nothing that troubles you?

LAURA: Nothing, Madame.

PERRODON: Well, you must know best. After so many years I hope that you keep nothing from me.

LAURA: Dear Madame Perrodon. Fetch your medicine. I promise to drink it like a good girl. Will that please you?

PERRODON: I am not so sure. Never before have you taken your medicine like a good girl.

She goes to the door.

LAURA: Madame . . .

PERRODON: Ah!

LAURA: Why had Papa to speak to the servants?

PERRODON: Why—to—to search for your friend, of course.

LAURA: Of course.

PERRODON *leaves her.*

Alone LAURA *puts her hand to her head and sways. She recovers herself, but the moment of weakness reminds her of last night's dream. She covers her face with her hands.*

Silently CARMILLA *enters and looks at* LAURA.

CARMILLA: Crying, dearest? With no one to comfort you?

LAURA: Carmilla?

CARMILLA: Take my hand.

She holds out her hand, but LAURA *does not take it.*

CARMILLA: Still independent.

LAURA: Where have you been?

CARMILLA: Would you believe me if I said that I did not know?

LAURA: I searched for you.

CARMILLA: I'm sure you did. Before I went to bed last night I locked my door as usual. This morning when I woke the door was wide open.

LAURA: Wilhelm forced the door when you didn't answer. The room was empty.

CARMILLA: Yet when I woke up, I was in my room again.

LAURA: The room was empty.

CARMILLA: Laura, my dear, I'm afraid.

LAURA: You?

CARMILLA: Something strange and terrible may have taken place.

LAURA: You know it did.

CARMILLA: I know nothing. sweetheart. Every night I close

my eyes and sink into darkness. But when I open my eyes this morning, I am bedeviled by mysteries. Doors are open that should be closed. There are strange looks from the servants, and you are in tears.

LAURA: You came to me.

CARMILLA: In my sleep?

LAURA: I don't know how. You were there, and . . . And . . . It was like the cold thrill we feel when we move against the current of a river. Darkness rising. And in the darkness, lips that kissed me. Longingly and more lovingly until they reached my throat . . . Then—nothing. But you were there.

CARMILLA: A dream, my precious. Nothing more.

LAURA: You have shared my dreams before.

CARMILLA: Seemed to, my pet. No more than seemed. We each dream our own dreams.

LAURA: You were there. You were there.

CARMILLA: Laura, my sweet . . .

LAURA: If you were not there, where were you?

CARMILLA: Perhaps I walked in my sleep . . . You don't believe me.

LAURA: I don't know. When I woke I could remember so little of what had happened. But I felt—corrupted.

CARMILLA: You should have called to me. I would have come to comfort you.

LAURA: No.

CARMILLA: Do you mean—no, you would never call, or no, I could not comfort you?

LAURA: I don't know.

CARMILLA: You mean you cannot trust me . . . Some words can hurt worse than knives.

LAURA: I'm sorry. But I know so little about you.

CARMILLA: Only that I am alone in a strange country.

LAURA: Not alone, Carmilla.

CARMILLA: Oh, my dear, if only I could tell you all that you want to know.

LAURA: Is it impossible?

CARMILLA: I have made solemn promises. If I tried to betray them now, the words would choke me.

LAURA (*flatly*): Your name is Carmilla. Your family is very ancient and noble. You have come a long way, and you have a long way to go.

CARMILLA: You are quite right to be bewildered and suspicious. But you can add one more item to that list. In the little time that I have known you, you have become dearer to me than anyone else in the world.

LAURA: Forgive me. I'm tired. (*She turns away.*)

CARMILLA: I think I must leave you.

LAURA: No.

CARMILLA: You have been very kind to me, you and your father. But I have already caused you too much trouble.

LAURA: I didn't mean that.

CARMILLA: Can a carriage be prepared for me? I know where my mother was going. I'll follow.

LAURA: You mustn't go.

CARMILLA: I'm used to travelling. It will be no great hardship.

LAURA: Carmilla!

CARMILLA: Do you think the carriage could be ready by tomorrow?

LAURA: I don't want you to go.

CARMILLA: It's for the best, little one. Suspicions have a habit of festering. I should rather leave you with happy memories.

LAURA: You mustn't leave at all.

CARMILLA: Even though I cause you pain?

LAURA: Even if . . . I don't know what to think. I'm so confused.

CARMILLA: There, there.

She puts her arm round LAURA's shoulders.

LAURA: I feel so—weak.

She begins to cry and buries her face against CARMILLA's shoulder.

CARMILLA: It will pass. Yes, there is pain, but there is sweetness too, and the pain is a small price for the sweetness. Don't worry. Soon you will know everything. Very soon now.

LAURA breaks away from her.

LAURA: That was foolish of me. I—I . . .

She crumples.

CARMILLA stands looking at her for a few seconds.

CARMILLA: We are of one kind, you and I, Laura. One blood.

Suddenly she hears someone approaching and kneels by LAURA.

CARMILLA (*waiting until she can be heard*): Laura!

MADAME PERRODON enters with a bottle and a glass.

PERRODON: And I have a bon-bon for . . . (*She stops with a cry on seeing LAURA.*)

CARMILLA *looks up at her.*

CARMILLA: Only a swoon, Madame. Girls are subject to them.

PERRODON: Mam'selle Laura. Mam'selle Laura. Imbecile that I was to bring the quinine, and not the smelling salts.

LAURA *stirs.*

PERRODON: Ah. She recovers.

LAURA: Madame? What—? You must not tell Papa.

PERRODON: There are some secrets, child, that cannot be kept.

LAURA: But I can stand now. Look.

With some assistance she gets to her feet.

PERRODON: I think you had better come to bed.

LAURA: But that's absurd. I was only dizzy for a moment.

PERRODON: Since when have you been dizzy, even for a moment? Take my arm, child.

LAURA: Madame . . .

PERRODON (*suddenly a governess again*): Take my arm.

She steers LAURA *towards the door.* LAURA *turns to* CARMILLA.

LAURA: Carmilla. You won't go, will you?

CARMILLA: Not without you, my dear.

PERRODON *and* LAURA *go out.*

CARMILLA: Not without you.

She follows them.

ACT TWO

Scene Two

THE TERRACE

Late afternoon. SMITHSON *strides angrily on to the terrace followed by* SPIELSBERG.

SMITHSON: A straight answer, man. Just give me a straight answer. You can speak out. We shan't be overheard here on the terrace.

DOCTOR: A fainting fit, no more. In my experience . . .

SMITHSON: To blazes with your experience. She's my daughter. She does not faint.

DOCTOR: I appreciate your concern, Colonel.

SMITHSON: There have been deaths in the village. The church bell hardly stops tolling.

DOCTOR: You can take my word, Colonel. There is no connection between your daughter's indisposition and the subjects of my report.

SMITHSON: Then why did she faint?

DOCTOR: The reasons for a young girl's swooning are legion—from a desire to be noticed to overtight stays.

SMITHSON: I can't laugh, man.

DOCTOR: I try to keep a sense of humour. Your daughter eats well, takes exercise, and sleeps with her window open.

SMITHSON: So?

DOCTOR: So there is nothing wrong with her.

FIELD (*off*): Signore.

SMITHSON: What the devil—?

The mountebank enters cautiously.

SMITHSON: How the devil did you get here?

FIELD: I read the 'ands of the servants.

SMITHSON: You'd better get off these premises double-quick.

FIELD: I help, maybe.

SMITHSON: I warned you last time I saw you ...

FIELD: The young lady, she sick.

DOCTOR: The young lady is not sick.

FIELD: I hear. But I expect, too. Like in the village.

DOCTOR: We have laws to protect us from rogues and vagabonds.

FIELD: They no protect from oupire.

DOCTOR: There is no oupire.

SMITHSON: Oupire?

DOCTOR: A figment of the imagination conjured by a charlatan for cheating the villagers.

FIELD: The young ladies no die of imagination, Dottore. The oupire have them.

SMITHSON: What is this oupire?

DOCTOR: The other word is vampire.

SMITHSON: Damned nonsense. I'm not having the women scared with these fairy tales. If you don't clear out, man, your bones are going to suffer for it.

FIELD: You gotta believe. The young lady she get weaker. Always the same with what you call vampire. I give proof, eh? There a little blue spot ere—justa below the throat. All the young lady that die 'ave it.

SMITHSON: Blue spot?

FIELD: Thata where vampires suck the life blood.

DOCTOR: If this creature is not put under restraint, Colonel, you'll have mass hysteria on your hands.

SMITHSON: A blue spot.

FIELD: I protect, eh?

DOCTOR: Now comes the rub. How much do you expect to extort from the Colonel?

FIELD: I aska nothing from the Colonel.

DOCTOR: A sophisticated rogue. It's enough to tell the villagers that the Colonel agrees with your clap-trap, and the money flows in faster than ever. It won't work, my friend. A fraud is still a fraud, and magistrates object to fraud.

FIELD: It's no fraud . . . Here come the young lady. You looka for blue spot, eh?

SMITHSON: If you so much as breathe the word vampire in my daughter's hearing, I'll have you thrashed.

FIELD: I no breathe, but you look.

LAURA *enters leaning on the arm of* CARMILLA. CARMILLA *is now obviously the stronger of the pair. She merely glances at the mountebank.* LAURA, *however, is delighted to see him.*

LAURA: Oh, you've come back.

FIELD: I never far away, signorina.

LAURA: Have you brought Beppo with you? Papa, he is is so funny with the puppet. (*She notices the stern looks of the men.*) Oh . . . I suppose you shouldn't be here.

FIELD: You no look, Colonel?

SMITHSON *is undecided, unsure of whether he is being made to look a fool.*

CARMILLA: How beautiful the sunset looks over the mountains.

FIELD: More beautiful than in Paris, eh?

CARMILLA: Red as blood. I wish I could paint.

FIELD: The signorina have other talents.

CARMILLA: The fortune-teller grows even bolder.

FIELD: Si. He take risk when risk have to be take. Colonel.

SMITHSON: Come here, my dear. The doctor wishes to—check something.

LAURA (*going over to the doctor*): The doctor looked at my tongue less than an hour ago. It's still here, Doctor.

She stumbles, and SMITHSON *leaps forward to support her.*

LAURA: How stupid of me. I can walk unaided, Papa.

DOCTOR: May I?

He pulls down the top of LAURA'S *dress slightly.*

There is a sharp intake of breath from the Colonel, and he looks across at FIELD, *shocked and bewildered.*

FIELD: A blue spot?

CARMILLA: These gypsies are clever, Colonel. They have ingenious ways of making you pay for what you already know. A little information is worth its weight in gold to them. How many guineas has the mountebank extorted from you on the strength of Laura's birthmark?

SMITHSON: Birthmark?

CARMILLA: I have one, too. A blue spot—here—on my throat. It is quite common among those of Karnstein blood. You wish to see it?

FIELD: But in the village . . .

CARMILLA: Have you seen this mark on any of the villagers, Doctor?

DOCTOR: No.

FIELD: That notta true.

DOCTOR: Permit me to believe the evidence of my own eyes.

FIELD: I give warning ...

CARMILLA: A threat now?

FIELD: No threat. I protect young lady.

DOCTOR: You are quite welcome to treat the patient ... In which case, of course, I accept no further responsibility.

FIELD: I no wanta quarrel. But if the young lady not take care ...

LAURA: What are you trying to say?

FIELD: The blue spot no birthmark. It vampire mark.

LAURA: Vampire?

SMITHSON: Get out! Get away from here before I break your neck with my own hands.

LAURA: Papa!

SMITHSON: Before morning there'll be a warrant out for your arrest. If you've half the cunning you're credited with, you'll be over the border before then.

FIELD: I go. I go.

DOCTOR: A move, my friend, you were advised to take earlier.

FIELD: I try ...

SMITHSON: Move!

Dejectedly the mountebank leaves.

LAURA: What did he mean?

SMITHSON: Gossip from the village. Feller tried to cadge on the strength of it.

LAURA: He said "vampire".

SMITHSON: Did he? Didn't hear very well myself.

LAURA: Oh, Papa. I thought you were about to strike him.

DOCTOR: Quite right, too. An insult to the intelligence.

CARMILLA: You do not believe in such things, Doctor?

DOCTOR: Do you?

CARMILLA shrugs her shoulders and turns to look out over the terrace again.

CARMILLA: The moon has risen already. She must be impatient for the night.

LAURA: Vampire? What did he mean?

SMITHSON: Another time, my dear. The sun's gone down. Chilly out here. You'd better come inside. You'll stay to dinner, of course, Spielsberg.

DOCTOR: A pleasure, Colonel. I should recommend a little wine for Miss Laura. Bring colour to her cheeks.

SMITHSON urges LAURA away, followed by the DOCTOR.

LAURA turns.

LAURA: Carmilla?

CARMILLA: In one moment. I should like to watch the last glimmer of daylight over the peaks.

LAURA: Don't be long.

CARMILLA is left alone.

CARMILLA: Ivan . . . Ivan.

In the distance a wolf howls.

CARMILLA: It will be soon, Ivan. Soon.

PERRODON bustles out on to the terrace.

PERRODON: Alone, Mam'selle? The night air is not good.

CARMILLA: I am not afraid of the night air, madame. Are you?

She leaves PERRODON.

PERRODON: Oui, mam'selle. There are many things of which Perrodon is afraid. Some of them may not even be spoken of.

FIELD (*in an urgent whisper off*): Madame.

PERRODON: Ah?

FIELD (*off*): Madame Perrodon.

PERRODON: Qui est là?

FIELD (*approaching*): The name does not matter, Madame.

PERRODON: The mountebank?

FIELD (*without the accent*): The mountebank will not be seen in these parts again.

PERRODON: Who are you, then?

FIELD: If you must know, Madame, the name is Field.

PERRODON: Field? Field! Ah!

FIELD: You've heard the name?

PERRODON: The Captain?

FIELD: I suppose I must be. I've not resigned my commission, nor been relieved of it.

PERRODON: But why—?

FIELD: It was important the monster shouldn't realise it had been discovered. It must not suspect until the time has come to strike.

PERRODON: But this garb . . .

FIELD: There'll be time enough for questions later. For now, you must trust me.

PERRODON: I do not know . . . What can I believe?

FIELD: All you need to believe, Madame, is that Miss Laura is in deadly danger—not merely of her life but of damnation.

PERRODON: Ah!

FIELD: I know, Madame. I know. I saw her cousin die. And the fiend that stole Beth's life is in this castle. She calls herself Carmilla.

PERRODON: Vous êtes fou, Captain Field. A wisp of a girl.

FIELD: With the bite of a snake. If only she could be crushed under heel like a viper.

PERRODON: You must not talk so. I do not know what you are doing here, or what you intend, but I think you should see the Colonel.

FIELD: In this garb, as you say? I shall. In my own time. As soon as I have discovered where the tomb is hidden. In the meantime what you have to do is simple.

PERRODON: I *have* to do nothing, Captain.

FIELD: You have to protect Miss Laura. Never leave her alone at night. During the day the murderess is a wisp of a girl. At night she is an invincible devil.

PERRODON: I know nothing of such things.

FIELD: My knowledge was dearly bought, Madame. I beg you to listen.

PERRODON: Well?

FIELD: For the next night or two, sleep in Miss Laura's room with her. Say she is too ill to be left alone. The Colonel will agree with you. Make sure that she wears a crucifix. Have garlic flowers in front of the window, and strew them on the bed.

PERRODON: Garlic?

FIELD: And pray that it keeps the vampire at bay.

PERRODON: Vampire?

FIELD: I've no more time, Madame. I must not be caught here. Take care of her, Madame.

PERRODON: Captain . . .

FIELD: Please.

PERRODON: Very well, I promise. It is little enough to do, even though you are mistaken, as I pray you are.

FIELD: Yes, pray, Madame. Pray. Prayers were never more needed.

He melts into the surrounding shadows.

PERRODON: Captain . . . Captain!

She goes a little way after him, but loses sight of him, and retraces her steps. She shivers.

CARMILLA: The night air is not good, Madame.

She glides into the light.

PERRODON: Oh.

CARMILLA: Surely you are not afraid of me, Madame?

PERRODON: Non. No, of course not.

CARMILLA: How bright the moon is. One is tempted to stay on the terrace here.

PERRODON: Oui.

CARMILLA: What a pity you were tempted, Madame.

PERRODON: It is cold now, though. We must go indoors.

CARMILLA: No, Madame. We must stay a little longer.

CARMILLA *stands between* PERRODON *and the castle. Whatever move the governess makes,* CARMILLA *is always between her and the door.*

PERRODON (*trying to exert an authority she does not feel*): Mam'selle Carmilla.

CARMILLA: A stupid name. A name for—a wisp of a girl.

PERRODON: Nevertheless it is your name, mam'selle.

CARMILLA: My name is Mircalla, Countess Karnstein.

PERRODON: I do not think that very humorous.

CARMILLA: Nor I, Madame.

PERRODON: The Countess died two hundred years ago. I have seen her picture.

CARMILLA: You have seen the original, Madame.

PERRODON: The Countess died, but did not die. What does that mean?

CARMILLA: You have heard of the undead?

PERRODON: There was talk in the village. I paid no attention.

CARMILLA: Not even when girls began to die? A pity, perhaps, but their blood was needed.

PERRODON: You?

CARMILLA: They would have died sooner or later anyway. All things must die. Except—some of us. And we have passed through death. But I need more than young blood. I can tell you, Madame, because I know you will not repeat a word.

PERRODON: I advise you to say nothing you may regret.

CARMILLA: I regret nothing. Only that after two hundred years one feels a hunger not even fresh blood can satisfy. The grave is a lonely place. I have always found myself travelling on alone. I thought that girl in Paris . . . It should have been so simple—like picking a flower. But an oaf of an officer . . .

PERRODON: C'est vrai!

CARMILLA: I shall not forget him. But this time—the Colonel will not allow his daughter's grave to be desecrated. I shall take Laura with me. She shall learn to feast with me—daintily—those pretty lips moist with living blood . . .

PERRODON: No!

CARMILLA: She is almost persuaded—even on this side of the grave. There is no-one to prevent it.

PERRODON: Non?

CARMILLA: But you do not count, Madame.

PERRODON: What do you intend?

CARMILLA: What can I do? I respect you, Madame Perrodon. But alas . . .

PERRODON: We shall see.

She tries to dash past CARMILLA, *but* CARMILLA *stretches out her hand and catches* PERRODON *round the throat.*

PERRODON *tries to tear the hand away, but* CARMILLA *has a grip like a steel trap.*

CARMILLA *looks sadly at* PERRODON *as the governess sinks to her knees, but it is almost as though that single hand were acting independently.*

CARMILLA: Je regrette, Madame.

ACT TWO

Scene Three

DRAWING-ROOM

In the darkness a bell tolls. Over it rises a cry that is almost a scream.

As the lights come up the bell continues.

CARMILLA *with her hands over her ears is trying to escape from the sound of the bell. She dashes about the room like a trapped bird.*

LAURA *comes into the room. She is now so weak that she can hardly walk.*

LAURA: Carmilla!

CARMILLA: That noise. That noise!

LAURA: It is the bell for Madame Perrodon.

CARMILLA: It drives me mad. Stop it. Stop it.

LAURA: We can't. She is to be buried here in the castle chapel, so the bell must be rung here.

CARMILLA: It beats inside my head.

LAURA (*putting her arm around* CARMILLA): Carmilla, dear.

CARMILLA: It's like whips, knives, fire . . .

LAURA: It's only a bell.

CARMILLA *screams in agony.*

The bell stops and CARMILLA *crumples, sobbing and shaking.*

LAURA: There, there. It's all over.

CARMILLA: Hold me.

LAURA: I'm here.

CARMILLA: Hold me tightly. Tightly. Don't leave me.

LAURA: I won't.

CARMILLA: Hold me.

LAURA: That's better, isn't it?

CARMILLA: The pain is passing . . . Oh, Laura, what should I do without you?

LAURA: Just as you did before you knew me, I suppose.

CARMILLA: Oh, no. Once I had met you, I knew that we could never be parted.

LAURA: It will happen some day. The bell will be rung for me. A few people will shed a few tears. Then it will be all over.

CARMILLA: Not for you, sweetheart. Not for you.

LAURA: I've been thinking about it in the last few days. I thought Madame Perrodon would be mourning for *me*.

CARMILLA: There will be no mourning for you, Laura.

LAURA: Not much, I hope. I shall be sorry to leave Papa all alone, but I shall be with Mama, and we shall all be united one day.

CARMILLA: You will be with me, Laura. With me.

LAURA: For a little while.

CARMILLA: For always.

LAURA: I wish it could be so, my dear. But you know that no one has ever recovered from this weakness.

CARMILLA: For you, my sweet, there will be a future more splendid than any you have dreamed of.

LAURA: Angels and golden harps?

CARMILLA: Don't mock me.

LAURA: I hadn't intended to. Here comes Papa. Let us try to deceive him, and convince him that I am well again.

SMITHSON *enters with the* DOCTOR. *The two men have just had another argument, and the truce will last as long as* LAURA *is in the room.*

SMITHSON: Blather, Spielsberg. A rigmarole to cover incompetence.

LAURA: Why, doctor. Here again? You'll soon have Papa asking if your intentions are honourable.

SMITHSON: You're looking a little better.

LAURA: I can't agree, Papa, without admitting that I have been ill. And I have not been ill, have I, Doctor?

DOCTOR: No symptoms that I could detect.

LAURA: I could not waltz if I were ill, could I? And I can . . .

But as she takes a step she collapses, and is caught by SMITHSON *who was expecting it.*

SMITHSON: To bed, my dear. I'll ring for one of the maids.

CARMILLA: There is no need, Colonel. I shall take Laura to her room.

LAURA: A few steps. I only wanted to take a few steps.

CARMILLA: Don't fret, my dear. Should I sleep in your room tonight?

LAURA: Oh, will you?

CARMILLA: I shall watch over you as you go to sleep.

LAURA: You're so good to me.

She is supported by CARMILLA *as they go out.*

When they are safely out of earshot, SMITHSON *turns on the* DOCTOR.

SMITHSON: You saw that. And you call yourself a doctor.

DOCTOR: Even soldiers have been known to lose battles.

SMITHSON: Lose? What d'you mean, lose? You're not throwing in your hand, are you?

DOCTOR: The pestilence must have been carried here from the village.

SMITHSON: I'm not interested in the how. What are you going to do about it?

DOCTOR: The treatment worked perfectly for Carmilla.

SMITHSON: Then it had better work for my daughter.

DOCTOR: Threats and bluster never yet cured anyone, Colonel.

SMITHSON: The day before yesterday you wouldn't even admit that she was ill.

DOCTOR: I admit, in that, I may have been mistaken.

SMITHSON: May have been? You're a bungler, sir. If you'd been in my regiment, I'd have had you cashiered.

DOCTOR: I shall prescribe a sedative.

SMITHSON: To keep the girl calm while the illness does its worst?

DOCTOR: For you, Colonel. Before you say any more that you may regret. If you wish to blame anyone, blame the mountebank. It was almost certainly he who introduced the plague to the castle.

SMITHSON: He'll be caught. The pity is he can only hang once—for Perrodon.

DOCTOR: Perrodon is the only one he has killed.

SMITHSON: Laura . . .

DOCTOR: Your daughter is still alive.

SMITHSON: You've as good as told me there's no hope.

DOCTOR: As long as the patient lives there is always hope.

SMITHSON: You're a humbug, sir. Worse, you're a canting hypocrite. Running with the hare and hunting with the hounds. As long as the fee's in your pocket, you don't give a damn for the patient. Worse. You'll go on trying to collect your fee until the bell has stopped tolling. Bloody vulture.

DOCTOR: I warned you, Colonel. I wash my hands of the case. Let us see if army medicine can cure your daughter.

He strides to the door, but there is confronted by FIELD *in full regimentals.*

The DOCTOR *blinks at him.*

DOCTOR: Don't I know you?

FIELD: Shouldn't think so, sir. Just arrived from Paris.

SMITHSON: Paris?

FIELD: Dashed laborious journey. Horse went lame. Delayed me. Apologise for crashing in like this, sir, but couldn't find any servants. Cooled my heels on the doorstep for a while, then marched in. Hope I haven't come at a dashed inconvenient time.

SMITHSON: My daughter's governess is to be buried in the chapel here tomorrow.

FIELD: What? I mean—deuced sorry, sir. Am I interrupting? Can come back later.

SMITHSON: The doctor was just about to leave.

FIELD: Evening, sir. See you again, perhaps.

DOCTOR: I doubt it.

He strides away.

FIELD *goes up to* SMITHSON *and salutes.*

FIELD: Colonel Smithson?

SMITHSON: Yes.

FIELD: Captain Field, sir.

SMITHSON: What?!

FIELD (*with less assurance*): Captain Field, sir.

SMITHSON: You have the effrontery to show your face here?

FIELD: Came as quickly as I could, sir. Had enquiries to make before I could present myself.

SMITHSON: Present yourself? A ghoul and a deserter?

FIELD: Not so, sir.

SMITHSON: I've had the reports. And don't tell me they were false—they were from the girl's father.

FIELD: I did what had to be done, sir.

SMITHSON: A stake was found hammered into the heart of the corpse. Damned desecration.

FIELD: Yes, sir.

SMITHSON: You don't deny it?

FIELD: The victim of a vampire becomes a vampire unless—precautions are taken.

SMITHSON: There's no such thing as a vampire.

FIELD: Beth died, sir. And your daughter is dangerously ill.

SMITHSON: What do you know about my daughter?

FIELD: I said I'd made enquiries, sir. I believe I know the whole story.

SMITHSON: If it's about vampires and such, you can keep it to yourself. I'm sick of these maunderings. Blue spots. Bloodsuckings...

FIELD: Unless I had been convinced, I should never have done what I did. But I must prove it, or I'm ruined. I shall only have proof if there is a witness with me when the monster is destroyed. I need your help, sir.

SMITHSON: I'll not be party to this mumbo-jumbo.

FIELD: But you'll hear me out, sir.

SMITHSON: Field, you're a sick man.

FIELD: Not as sick as your daughter, sir.

SMITHSON: The doctor says there's hope—even though the man is a fool.

FIELD: He's no fool, sir. I wish he were. It would explain so much that needs to be explained. He knows what is happening in the village. Why does he deny it?

SMITHSON: At least he's more sense than to believe in hippogriffs and unicorns.

FIELD: I travelled once through Transylvania, sir. I know what I saw there. I could never forget it. I realise that what I say will distress you; but will you refuse to listen when it may save your daughter?

SMITHSON: Get on with it then.

FIELD: Years ago a woman in this district had two lovers, and she didn't give a damn for either of them. She played them against each other until one of them killed himself. His family was well-connected, and for a while at least he was saved from a suicide's grave. But, under certain circumstances, a suicide can become one of the undead. He attacked the woman, and she, too, died. Worse, she became a vampire in her turn. The dead lover was dealt with. His body was dug up and the stake hammered home.

SMITHSON: And the woman?

FIELD: The remaining lover was still faithful. Evil though she was he could not bear to think of the stake in her heart. He made sure that she was buried in an unmarked tomb. She has lain undisturbed since then. Her name was Mircalla, Countess Karnstein.

SMITHSON: That I won't believe. My wife was a Karnstein. My daughter is a Karnstein.

FIELD: The truth can't be changed to suit convenience, sir.

SMITHSON: How is it that no word has ever come down to me? I've all the family papers here.

FIELD: But you haven't read them, sir.

SMITHSON: Not in my line. But Spielsberg has. He's been through every one. He's never even mentioned a Mircalla.

FIELD: Don't you wonder why, sir? He had the records to

his hand. I had to piece together and sift through half-forgotten stories and whispered rumours. He had evidence in black and white while I was scraping moss from old stones—to find the tomb without a name. Don't you wonder why he has never spoken? But I've one piece of evidence that you may recognise, sir.

SMITHSON: Well, sir?

FIELD: It seems that a vampire can change its name, but is forced to retain the letters. In Paris the Countess was known as Millarca. Here her name is Carmilla.

SMITHSON: Damnit, no!

FIELD: I saw her in Paris. I've seen her here.

SMITHSON: But she's with my daughter now.

FIELD: No, sir. Her shape is with your daughter. Her body is in that tomb. Will you come with me, sir, and see the creature destroyed?

SMITHSON: I can't believe it. I'll speak to the girl now.

FIELD: No, sir. Frighten it away now and someday the scourge will return.

SMITHSON: But my daughter's in danger.

FIELD: I'm afraid so, sir. Unless the vampire is annihilated. I doubt if your daughter will see the sun rise tomorrow.

SMITHSON: You may be right. You may be wrong. But will you give me your word of honour that you believe this to be true?

FIELD: My honour is at stake, sir.

SMITHSON: I'll come with you.

FIELD: Thank you, sir. We haven't much time. We can only destroy the body during daylight. Once night falls the creature is indestructible.

SMITHSON: Then don't just stand there. Hurry, man. Hurry.

He rushes out, sweeping FIELD *along with him.*

ACT TWO

Scene Four

THE DRAWING-ROOM

CARMILLA *and* LAURA *enter together.* LAURA *is nearly exhausted.*

LAURA: I can't go any further.

CARMILLA: Rest, then. There is plenty of time.

LAURA: Why should you want to take me down to the chapel?

CARMILLA: There is something I must show you in the chapel.

LAURA: I'm not sure that I want to go. Madame Perrodon is lying there.

CARMILLA: You were not afraid of her while she was alive. Why should you be afraid now that she is dead?

LAURA: I'm not afraid, but I feel that we are—intruding.

CARMILLA: She will not complain.

LAURA: Don't—please—don't sound so heartless.

CARMILLA: Everyone must die. It's quite natural.

LAURA: Of course. But for a little while they should have—respect.

CARMILLA: Then we shall pay our respects to Madame Perrodon.

LAURA: But it seems such a long way, and I'm so tired. Even when we get there, we must come back again.

CARMILLA: You need not worry about coming back again.

LAURA: What do you mean?

CARMILLA: I mean that I am with you. I shall be with you always.

LAURA: Dear Carmilla. Such a little while ago you were depending on me.

CARMILLA: I still depend upon you, my sweet. I shall always depend upon you. Are you ready to walk a little further?

LAURA: We shall have to rest again on the next landing. I can hardly put one foot in front of the other.

CARMILLA: Tomorrow that will be past. I promise.

LAURA: You can't tell.

CARMILLA: Laura—what is happening to you now, happened once to me. You will recover as I did. You will become stronger than ever you were before. Nothing will ever harm you again. Are you ready?

CARMILLA supports LAURA as they walk on.

ACT TWO

Scene Five

THE KARNSTEIN RUINS

Early evening. There is the sound of hammers on stone.

SMITHSON (*off*): Steady there. Now heave. Heave. It's moving. There.

There is a crash as a heavy piece of stone falls. Then a cry from FIELD.

FIELD (*off*): Oh, God!

FIELD hurries in looking about him as though searching for something.

FIELD: Empty. Empty.

SMITHSON *follows him.*

SMITHSON: Steady, man.

FIELD: It was empty. The tomb was empty.

SMITHSON: I saw it.

FIELD: It had to be her tomb. It was the only tomb without a name. Is there another? There can't be another.

SMITHSON: In my opinion it's never been used.

FIELD: A blind. A trap for fools like me who thought they knew everything. But this is the Karnstein vault. She must be here somewhere. Under another name perhaps.

SMITHSON: What now?

FIELD: We've so little time. The sun's already settling behind the ruins. Break open another tomb. Use the little time we have doing something.

SMITHSON: Save your strength. You might just as well try to topple these walls. You were wrong, Captain. Admit it. There are no walking dead here. Never were.

FIELD: There is evil here. There is. Can't you feel it?

SMITHSON: You can find evil anywhere, young feller, if you look hard enough. In my experience it comes parcelled up as men. Nothing so fancy as vampires. I'll tell Karl and Ludwig to pack up the tools.

FIELD: It's here. I know it. (*Shouting.*) Come out. I know you're here. Come out.

The DOCTOR *saunters towards them.*

DOCTOR: How very perceptive, Captain.

SMITHSON: You followed us.

DOCTOR: The prospect amused me—Colonel Smithson, that leader of men, following a will-o'-the-wisp.

FIELD: You didn't follow us or we'd have seen you. You were here before us. You knew we'd come here.

DOCTOR: Where else in these parts would one pursue a vampire?

FIELD: You know she's here.

DOCTOR: You have the advantage over me, Captain. Regrettably I don't believe in vampires.

SMITHSON: Do you believe in anything?

DOCTOR: I believe in hygiene and sanitation.

FIELD: I too, Doctor. But those girls in the village were killed by a vampire.

DOCTOR: Modern science denies the existence of such a creature.

SMITHSON: Oh, don't waste time here.

FIELD: Waste time, Colonel? We may lose the murderer, but we have the accessory. You knew what was happening, Spielsberg.

DOCTOR: I? The symptoms conformed to nothing in the text-book—general weakness, blue spots . . .

FIELD: You denied ever seeing a blue spot.

SMITHSON: So he did.

DOCTOR: It's not for me to advance superstition. Admit one grain of truth in their myths and years of progress will be swept away. Medicine replaced by magic again.

FIELD: You knew what was happening, and you denied it.

DOCTOR: I still deny it.

FIELD: Even though you know.

DOCTOR: I know nothing.

FIELD: You learned nothing from the Karnstein papers?

DOCTOR: Births, deaths, and marriages.

FIELD: Nothing of Mircalla, Countess Karnstein? Where she is buried?

DOCTOR: What does it matter where she is buried?

FIELD: You know, Doctor. You know.

DOCTOR: There is no such thing as a vampire.

FIELD: But you know where the Countess is buried.

DOCTOR (*shrugging his shoulders*): I know.

FIELD: Where? In which of these graves?

SMITHSON: Well, man?

DOCTOR: A typical request, Colonel. Barked with all the grace of an order to a whipped cur.

SMITHSON: What the devil are you talking about?

DOCTOR: You dismissed me today with the same courtesy. I suggest you apply for information to your new physician.

SMITHSON: If Laura dies, man, I'll personally put a bullet through your head.

FIELD: You can save yourself a charge of murder, Colonel. In Transylvania I saw what was left of a man suspected of harbouring a vampire. He'd been torn to pieces.

DOCTOR: We boast a veneer of civilisation here, Captain.

FIELD: It may crack when the villagers remember what happened to their women. Karl's daughter was one of the first. Karl!

DOCTOR: Wait!

FIELD: Where is the tomb of the Countess Millarca?

DOCTOR: It is described in the Colonel's documents. Consult them.

FIELD: You spent years sifting through them. We have until the sun goes down behind the mountains.

SMITHSON: Karl.

DOCTOR: Can you reach the castle before night falls, Captain?

FIELD: Three miles away?

DOCTOR: Because the body of the Countess lies in the chapel there. Remember your wife was a Karnstein. It seems that all these years you have been harbouring a vampire, Colonel. If you believe in such things.

SMITHSON: Damn you!

He runs out calling to the servants.

SMITHSON: Where are the horses? Bring them over here.

FIELD: Go back to Vienna, Doctor. You'll find it healthier there.

SMITHSON (*off*): Field!

FIELD: Coming, Colonel.

He runs out after the Colonel.

DOCTOR: I could have lied. Why didn't I lie?

He shrugs his shoulders and walks away. The sound of horses hooves start and fade.

ACT TWO

Scene Six

THE CHAPEL IN THE CASTLE

The fading light falls through a stained glass window.

CARMILLA *enters supporting* LAURA.

LAURA: It's almost dark.

CARMILLA: I can still see daylight through the stained window. Night creeps on so slowly.

LAURA (*glancing back*): Madame Perrodon...

CARMILLA: Hush. Hush.

LAURA: So still.

CARMILLA: Are you afraid to die?

LAURA: A little. Everyone is.

CARMILLA: But to die together so as to be together always.

LAURA: I don't understand.

CARMILLA: You will, my sweet. In a little while. In a very little while.

LAURA: Why have you brought me here?

CARMILLA: Just a little further.

LAURA: I'm so tired.

They pause before a solid block of masonry.

CARMILLA: This is where you will rest, sweetheart.

LAURA: I?

CARMILLA: You and I together.

LAURA: It's a tomb.

CARMILLA: Undisturbed for two hundred years. It shall be undisturbed now for eternity.

LAURA (*turning away*): I don't want to look.

CARMILLA: Only because you cling to a shred of mortality. I shall make you immortal.

LAURA (*stumbling away from the tomb*): I remember now. I remember the dream.

CARMILLA: And in the dream you offered your blood.

LAURA: I—?

CARMILLA: Freely. Willingly. Because love must have sacrifices and sacrifices demand blood.

LAURA: My—blood?

CARMILLA: Soon now. Soon. When the last glimmer of daylight fades from your hair.

LAURA: Must I?

CARMILLA: If you love me.

LAURA: I thought my dream was evil. I felt corrupted.

CARMILLA: Am I evil? Am I corrupt?

LAURA: You are beautiful, Carmilla.

CARMILLA: You are beautiful, Laura. And you shall be beautiful for ever. The moment has almost come. Do you surrender yourself freely?

LAURA (*drowsily*): Freely.

CARMILLA: Willingly?

LAURA: Willingly.

CARMILLA takes LAURA in her arms. There is a sudden clatter outside.

SMITHSON (*off*): Kick the door open, man. It's not locked.

FIELD: In here?

SMITHSON: In. In.

SMITHSON and FIELD run in. SMITHSON carries a wooden stake and hammer in one hand, and a flambeau or candelabrum in the other.

FIELD holds an enormous crucifix which obviously belongs to the chapel.

With a hiss, CARMILLA pushes LAURA from her.

FIELD advances holding up the crucifix. CARMILLA backs

away from FIELD *towards the tomb.* FIELD *forces her down on to the tomb.*

He throws his cloak over CARMILLA, *covering her completely.*

FIELD: Colonel.

SMITHSON, *whose attention has been distracted towards* LAURA, *hurries over to* FIELD.

FIELD *lays the crucifix on the cloak and takes the stake and hammer from the Colonel.*

LAURA: No. No!

SMITHSON *hurries back to* LAURA.

FIELD *sets the stake against the shape under the cloak and raises the hammer.*

LAURA: Carmilla.

FIELD *brings down the hammer on to the stake.*

There comes a scream that echoes round the chapel.

FIELD: As I promised, Countess.

LAURA: Carmilla.

She staggers towards the tomb, but SMITHSON *holds her back.*

SMITHSON: No, my dear.

LAURA: Let me go to her.

SMITHSON: Better not.

LAURA: You killed her. You killed her.

FIELD: She would have killed you, miss.

LAURA: That doesn't matter.

FIELD: She was evil.

LAURA: She was beautiful.

FIELD *pulls away his cloak revealing a wizened body with a few rags clinging to it. He picks up a skull covered with whisps of grey hair.*

FIELD: This is your beauty, miss.

LAURA *reacts as though to a blow.*

LAURA: You—did—that—to her?

She turns to the colonel with a sob, then pulls herself together.

LAURA: Take me away, Papa.

SMITHSON *puts his arm round her and supports her towards the door.*

There he pauses and turns to FIELD.

FIELD: She's laughing. Even in hell she's laughing.

The colonel goes out, leaving the place in darkness.

CURTAIN